RVing Tips, Tricks And Techniques

A Collection Of Columns And Articles

written by

D1557381

Joe and Vicki Kieva

I

RVing Tips, Tricks And Techniques

First Printing 2001

ISBN # 0-9655620-3-4

Published by RV Travel Adventures
P.O. Box 5055
Huntington Beach, CA 92615

www.rv know how.com

Printed in the United States of America

About The Authors

Joe and Vicki Kieva, whose 35 years of RVing experience has taken them throughout the United States, Canada and Mexico, are probably the RVing community's best known speaking and writing team.

Since 1993, Joe and Vicki have been sharing their knowledge and experience by presenting "how-to" seminars and classes at RV shows, rallies, and educational events across the country (and logging over 20,000 RVing miles a year in the process).

Each month, Joe and Vicki's popular RV advice columns and articles are published in the Good Sam Club's *Highways* magazine and Woodall Publication's seven regional *RV Traveler* magazines.

This book, in addition to an assortment of tip trivia, is a collection of some of those columns and articles.

Contents

Contents

We have two credit cards; each from a different bank. Joe carries the credit card of one bank in his wallet. I carry the credit card of the other bank in mine. Neither of us carries both credit cards. That way, if one of us loses a wallet, and we have to cancel the credit card in that wallet, we can use the remaining, still-valid credit card in the other person's wallet.

On hot sunny days, try to select a campsite that points the front of your RV towards the east or south. Your RV's entry-door wall can be protected from the hot afternoon sun by the patio awning. The opposite side-wall will be the naturally shady side of your rig during most of the day.

An RVer who uses campground laundry rooms can't have too many quarters. Save your quarters in a 35mm film canister. Each canister holds approximately $7.00 worth of quarters and makes a convenient spill-proof container.

Expert Opinions

"You could make life a lot easier for me if you would just tell me what kind of RV you and the other "RV experts" have and how they are equipped."

Joe: OK! But I don't think the answer will make life easier for you.

During a University of Idaho's "Life On Wheels" Conference, Vicki and I were among 12 "RV Experts" who participated as panel members in an RV Lifestyle forum.

Among the panel participants were: a single, full-timing woman; a single (now married) full-timing man; two full-timing couples; a couple who had fulltimed for many years but are now extended travelers and two couples (including Vicki and I) who travel extensively in their RVs but are not fulltimers.

For the sake of discussion we'll say there were three extended travelers and four full timers; with a total of seven RVs.

Two extended travelers and the full-timing woman have Class A motorhomes. Each tows a small car.

The extended travelers who used to be fulltimers have a Class C motorhome. They do not tow a transportation vehicle.

The full-timing man and one full-timing couple have fifth-wheel trailers with one or more slideout rooms. One tows with a medium duty tow vehicle; the other tows with a pickup truck.

The remaining full-timing couple has a fifth-wheel without a slideout room. They also tow with a pickup truck.

2

One of the Class A motorhomes and all of the fifth-wheel tow vehicles are powered by diesel engines.

Vicki: All the full-timing RVers and one extended traveler have their rigs equipped with solar panels and inverters. The two remaining extended travelers don't see any need for them. Interestingly, the extended travelers without the solar panels prefer boondocking and government campgrounds while one full-timing couple with solar panels favor commercial campgrounds with full hookups.

Two fulltimers belong to membership campground organizations. The remainder do not.

Preferences in overnight accommodations depended upon each RVer's interests, needs and budget at the moment. None of us stayed exclusively in any one type of campground.

Only one extended traveler and one full-timing couple travel with a pet.

Only one fulltiming and one extended traveler have a washer/dryer in their RV. One fulltimer claimed she washes her clothes on a rock!

As the panel continued to answer questions posed by the audience, it was obvious that we all had equally diverse opinions and preferences when it came to the various aspects of choosing, using and enjoying our RVs.

One thing we all agreed on though. We love the feeling of independence and the sense of freedom we get from traveling and living in an RV

Joe: So you see, whatever type of RV you choose, however you equip it, wherever or however you camp, you'll be doing exactly what the experts do.

Budget Start

"We are in our late twenties and have two pre-school children. We recently purchased a low-mileage Ford Explorer and would like to try camping in a trailer. The prices for the trailers we saw at an RV show are more than we can afford. How does someone on a tight budget manage to become an RVer?"

Joe: You don't have to invest a great deal of money to become an RVer. We suggest you start by shopping for a small, inexpensive, used trailer.

A Ford Explorer can probably tow a trailer that weighs in the neighborhood of 5,000 pounds. Contact a Ford dealer or the manufacturer to determine exactly how much weight your particular vehicle is rated to tow. If you get a trailer that weighs less than 3,500 pounds empty, you will be able to add up to 1,500 pounds of water, propane and camping gear. Keep in mind, though, that the lighter and smaller the trailer, the easier it will be for your tow vehicle to handle it.

Chances are you will only be using your trailer for occasional weekend camping trips and a two or three week vacation. All you really need is a warm, dry place for you and your kids to eat, sleep and keep your stuff.

Folding trailers (also known as pop-ups or tent trailers) can be easily towed by a sport utility vehicle. They are small enough to fit in almost any campsite and may even be light enough to push around by hand. Fully set up they will sleep four to six people comfortably.

Travel trailers up to 20 feet will have couches, dinettes and, in some models, overhead cabinets that will do double duty by unfolding into sleeping accommodations. Most will have a small galley and bath.

Many years ago, we traveled around the country with three small kids in a 17-foot travel trailer. After dinner, everyone had to go outside while I converted the trailer into a bedroom. Before breakfast, everyone went outside again so I could convert it back to a kitchen and living area.

If your fully loaded trailer is heavier than 1,500 pounds, it should have electric brakes, and I would suggest equipping the tow vehicle with a weight-distributing hitch and an auxiliary transmission cooler.

When you locate a trailer that is in your price range and will satisfy your needs, notice if it shows pride of ownership. A carelessly treated living area may indicate more critical areas have not been maintained. Stained ceilings or wall panels are signs of leaks and water damage. Look for structural damage to the roof, sides and undercarriage. Test and examine the propane, electric, water and sewer systems. Before you buy, you might even want to have an RV service technician check out the trailer and give you an estimate to repair any discrepancies he discovers.

Vicki: You don't have to spend a fortune to equip your trailer. Most of our first trailer's pots, pans, dishes and kitchen utensils came from yard sales.

Sleeping bags for each member of the family do not have to be expensive, either. You are not going to be carrying them on your back, nor will you be sleeping on the ground. An extra blanket or quilt can always be added on cold nights.

National, state, and county parks offer no-frills campsites in natural settings at very reasonable prices. Commercial campgrounds usually have more amenities and their prices will reflect their investment. Ask your campground neighbors if they know of any budget-priced campgrounds in the area. Join the Good Sam RV Club. It is the best information resource available to RVers. Membership will get you a ten percent discount at campgrounds all over the country. Get a *Trailer Life RV Park and Campground Directory*. It lists, describes and rates campgrounds and RV parks. Use it to locate campgrounds that fit your budget. Subscribe to *Trailer Life* magazine. It provides a wealth of practical, useful information to trailer owners. Call 800-234-3450 for more information about the Good Sam Club, Trailer Life magazine and the campground directory.

So, go ahead. Buy a small inexpensive trailer. Take your family camping. Build memories. Some day you'll realize it was the best investment you ever made.

If you spread a half dozen fabric softener sheets throughout the interior of your RV before putting it in storage, it will have a fresh smell when you open it up again.

Tire valve caps, especially those on inside duals, will be easier to grip and hold onto if you slip a short length of tubing (fuel line works great) over the cap while you are removing or installing it.

6

Smaller RVs

"We are in our late-twenties and have one child. Both of us are involved in our careers and enjoy tent camping. Our jobs are such that we are frequently able to take three and four day weekends in addition to an annual three week vacation. We're shopping for a self-propelled RV. Everyone seems to think we should get a large motorhome. What do you think?"

Joe: I think you should take a close look at your personal interests, needs and budget. Where do you want to go? What do you want to do? Who will be going? How often will you use the RV? How much do you want to spend? The answers to these questions should help you zero in on the type and size RV that will satisfy your interests, needs and budget.

Vicki: Yours is an instance where smaller may be smarter. Look seriously at the smaller (up to 24 feet) motorhomes, van conversions and slide-in truck campers. Since you're accustomed to tent-camping, you'll appreciate the advantages (sleeping above ground level, screen windows, solid roof and walls) of the smaller RVs and not miss the luxuries (hydraulic levelers, washer/dryer, ice-maker) of the larger motorhomes.

You'll find that smaller RVs have a number of advantages. Most are not much bigger than a full-size car so they are easy to drive and maneuver. They'll take you every place the larger RVs can go and a number of places where the bigger rigs won't fit.

Most smaller RVs are well within the size and weight restrictions that may be posted on roads, bridges and tunnels. You'll also find it easier to find parking space in shopping centers and tourist attractions.

Your smaller rig will fit in all of a campground's sites instead of just the larger ones. And, if you're not towing anything, you won't care if the campsite is a back-in or pull-through.

Joe: Smaller RVs can be time efficient. You can leave a campground in the morning and visit tourist attractions in a crowded city. Then, because you don't have to return to the previous night's campground to retrieve your RV, you can continue down the road to your next destination.

When you take off for a day trip you won't have to transfer coolers, cameras and clothes from an RV to a car or truck (and hope you haven't forgotten anything).

Less rig means less stuff to load and unload. It also means less vehicle to clean. Because it's less trouble, you'll be more inclined to take that RV on day trips to the beach and quick overnight outings.

And, mid day at a tourist attraction, you can retreat to your home-on-wheels for lunch, a change of clothes or a brief nap.

Depending upon the vehicle's gross combined weight rating, you may be able to tow a small trailer. You'll have the option of towing a boat, motorcycle or, if your family grows, a tent trailer.

Vicki: A van conversion or truck-camper also provides the financial advantage of being utilized as a second transportation vehicle. It can be used for commuting, taking the dog to the vet, hauling garden supplies and family transportation. By the way, there's nothing like a child to make you appreciate having a bathroom in your transportation vehicle.

Purchase price, vehicle registration fees, insurance, repairs and maintenance will probably be less than that of larger vehicles. At this stage of your life, saving for your child's college education or a down payment on a house may have a higher priority than having a luxury coach.

Joe: Or, you may prefer a rig with hydraulic levelers, washer/dryer and an ice-maker. In which case ....

A propane fired furnace can devour a lot of propane on a cold night. Once it has taken the chill out of the interior of your rig, switch over to a portable electric heater. It will maintain your rig at a comfortable temperature for a considerable amount of time.

Roughing It

"It's obvious your current RV is a large, comfortable, motorhome. How long has it been since you went "roughing it" in a small camper or trailer?"

Joe: We bought our first RV in 1963. It was a 13-foot trailer with years of experience. A sleeping platform with a thin mattress stretched across the rear wall. It was not much wider than a single bed but we were younger and thinner then.

A booth-type dinette at the front of the trailer could be converted into a one-person bunk. There was a small storage area under each of the dinette seats.

The kitchen consisted of a single sink and a two burner propane stove. There was an icebox and storage cupboard underneath.

Water came from a five-gallon jerry can with a faucet near the bottom. I filled the can at the campground spigot and then set it on the kitchen sideboard so its faucet hung over the the sink. The sink water drained through a hose and into a bucket outside.

It was a perfect camping rig. It never occurred to us that we might be "roughing it".

In 1966 we moved up to a brand-new 17-foot trailer. The gaucho couch, dinette and two fold-down bunks provided sleeping accommodations for our family of five.

The kitchen had a 4-burner range, oven and small propane/electric refrigerator. There was also a tiny commode room. It had a 20-gallon fresh-water tank. One 17-gallon holding tank captured both gray and black water.

At night, everyone stepped outside while dad converted the trailer into a bunkhouse. In the morning, everyone went outside again so the trailer could be made into a cook-shack. That trailer made camping so easy that we took our kids on a five-month trip around the United States in it. We bought a nicely equipped 24-foot Class C motorhome in 1981. 80,000 miles later we traded the Class C for a 32-foot Class A and after 110,000 miles, we purchased our first diesel pusher.

Vicki: Your letter made us wonder if we could handle "roughing it" in a smaller RV. We borrowed an 11- foot camper mounted on a properly equipped pickup truck. Our destination? Undecided, but somewhere in the Sierra Mountains of California.

The camper might be called an 11-footer but, in fact, the floor was 11-feet, 6 inches long and the cabover added another eight feet to the overall length.

It featured a queen size bed, 3-way, 6-cubic foot refrigerator; 3-burner stove; propane oven; microwave oven; thermostat-controlled, forced air furnace; 6-gallon water heater; roof-mounted air-conditioner; AM/FM CD player and a television set.

Somehow they also managed to squeeze in a 40-gallon fresh-water tank, 25-gallon gray water tank and 24-gallon black water tank. Did I mention that it had a generator?

Best of all, the camper had a bathroom with sink, commode and a surprisingly roomy separate shower.

We agreed we could "rough it" in a camper like this.

Joe: The truck had no problem getting us up to interstate speed. Climbing into the Sierras was a breeze.

I expected the camper to roll over on its side when I went around corners but the dual wheels, adjustable air bags and adjustable shocks seemed to eliminate that tendency. The stabilizing effect of the suspension system was especially appreciated in the strong desert crosswinds we encounted during that trip. The smaller dimensions of the truck and camper allowed us to push into the backroad country. We maneuvered easily along narrow dirt roads and through tight Forestry Service campgrounds. That would have been a challenge in our larger motorhome. Size of our RV was not a consideration when we selected a secluded campsite.

Vicki: We cooked our dinner over an open fire for the first time in many years. But, we retreated behind the protection of the camper's screened door and windows in order to eat and not be eaten. So much for "roughing it".

That night, instead of listening to the roar of interstate traffic, rumbling trains or planes taking off, we fell asleep to the sounds of a rushing mountain stream. It had been a long time.

The next day we wandered into a commercial RV park with full hookups. We connected to electric, water, sewer and cable TV. The desert turned hot. We turned on the air-conditioning and finished an article on our laptop. After e-mailing the article at the campground's modem hookup we drove the camper to a Basque restaurant and had dinner.

Choosing the size and type of RV you own involves compromising between space and agility. For some, full-timing or extended travel might be more comfortable in a larger motorhome or trailer. For others, weekends and vacations or excursions involving narrow roads might be a lot easier in something smaller. One thing is for sure, RVing in a camper does not mean having to "rough it."

Buying a Larger RV

"We are considering trading in our 24 foot motorhome on one in the 30 - 32 foot range. We particularly enjoy camping in government campgrounds. Will we encounter any size problems with the larger rig?"

Joe: Our previous motorhome was 32 feet long. We found that most major national, state and county campgrounds could readily accommodate RVs up to 32 feet. Obviously, the higher into the mountains or the deeper into the forest, the fewer campgrounds and campsites we could fit into.

Our present motorhome is 36 feet long. During the last couple of years we have stayed in a number of national and state campgrounds. While there were sites large enough to accommodate the larger RVs, there were even more sites that would accommodate a 32 foot or smaller RV.

Vicki: Think about the types of government campgrounds you are attracted to. The height and width of the 32 footer will probably be no more of a consideration than your current motorhome. The length, however, may limit the number of campsites that you can fit into. The length may also affect your ability to navigate the narrow roads and sharp turns of some older, more remote campgrounds.

Use your campground directories to look up the kind of government campgrounds you plan to frequent. See if they have any size limitations that would preclude the size RV you are considering.

You may find, as we did, that a 32-foot RV will take you where you want to go and let you do the things you want to do.

Wide Bodies, Narrow Roads

"The Trailer Life Campgrounds, RV Parks and Services Directory indicates that a lot of states have an eight-foot width limitation. Does this mean that wide-body RVs are not legal in these states? If so, how does everybody avoid getting tickets? You can't always stay on a major highway."

Joe: One of the biggest surprises (and disappointments) many owners of large RVs experience is when they discover there are campgrounds, bridges and highways that cannot accommodate their rigs. They are just too big.

The campground situation is easy. If there is a size limitation, it is usually noted in the campground directory. That same directory can be used to locate another nearby campground that has no such restrictions.

Bridges with weight limitations generally have them posted before reaching the bridge. If you are lucky, there is an alternate route or a turnaround spot available.

But, vehicle width restrictions on highways are a more complicated matter. Laws pertaining to the width of motor vehicles vary from state to state. They are subject to change, rarely posted on the highway, not readily available to the tourist and frequently confusing.

There are exceptions, but here is what we have observed about these laws:

Widths up to 96 inches (standard-width RVs) are generally permitted on all federal and state highways.

Widths up to 102 inches (wide-body RVs) are generally permitted on all federal interstate highways.

Widths up to 102 inches are permitted on designated state highways in most states. Each state has its own way of identifying its designated state highways. Most fall into the categories of divided highways, highways with four or more lanes, or highways with lanes at least 12 feet wide (as narrow as 10 feet in a few states). But, just because a highway falls into one of those categories, does not necessarily mean it is a designated state highway.

Counties and cities are also permitted to establish width limitations for their own roads and highways.

Please note that we used the words generally and exceptions. Our observations are certainly general and there most certainly are exceptions.

Vicki: So what happens if you innocently drive your wide-body RV on a highway that has a 96-inch width limitation? Will you get a traffic ticket? It's possible. Ignorance of the law, we've heard, is no excuse.

The real concern, we think, is what happens if your wide-body RV is involved in an accident while traveling on that highway. What if the size of your rig is a contributing factor in that accident? How will the courts react? How will your insurance company respond?

Trip planning for those of us who own wide-bodies (RVs, not torsos) should include determining which wide-body-friendly highways are available to take us to our destination.

Easier said than done. Realistically speaking, not too many of us have the time or inclination to contact the various government jurisdictions to determine which roads are wide-body legal.

So we jump onto the road and take our chances. We feel comfortable on the interstates and the major state highways, especially in the company of all those 102-inch wide tractor-trailers. If they are legal, we think, we must be too.

And we don't feel too nervous about driving on divided, multi-laned, major state highways. With any luck they fall into the "designated highways" that permit wide-bodies.

We do feel concerned, though, when we travel on the narrower state and county roads. There is a very good chance it is one that has a 96-inch width limitation. This is especially true in the eastern states where roads were laid out many years ago for much smaller and slower vehicles.

Joe: Last summer we drove our 102-inch wide motorhome across the width of a small eastern state. The two-lane country road had been recommended by locals as an especially scenic route. They were right. It was spectacular. But, too late, we discovered it was also very narrow. There were times when, looking in the side view mirrors, I could see either the roadway's painted center line or the curb line, but not both at the same time. And there were times when there were no lines on the road at all.

Obviously, our motorhome was too wide for that byway. If we had met an oncoming eight-foot wide vehicle, somebody would have had to drive on the shoulder. Fortunately we met only a few oncoming cars. The trucks were smart enough to take another route.

Another reason to have avoided that road was the weight restrictions on its many small bridges. The weight limit was 16 tons. Our motorhome weighed 28,000 pounds that day, but it could have weighed more. I wonder when those bridges were last inspected and deemed fit to support 16 tons.

We did not get a ticket that day, nor were we involved in an accident. We lucked out. Legal or not, lucky or not, we should not have been on that road. We were too big; it was not safe. Next time we'll think to ask about the width of the road. If the pavement isn't at least 24 feet wide, we'll park the motorhome, enjoy the scenic road in our car and continue our RV journey on the interstates.

When we went from a motorhome that was 32-feet long and 96 inches wide to one 36-feet long and 102-inches wide, we knew there were places we would no longer be able to go. Our RV would just be too big. When it came to compromising between mobility and living accommodations, we deliberately chose livability.

Vicki: How does the owner of a wide body avoid getting tickets? By avoiding the roads and highways that prohibit wide bodies. How do we know if it prohibits wide bodies? Do a little research, add common sense and hope you are lucky.

Driving Large RVs

"My wife and I have been enjoying weekends and vacations in an 18-foot travel trailer for five years. We will retire soon and plan to spend two to three months a year touring North America in a motorhome. A larger RV makes sense for what we want to do but I'm not sure I would be comfortable driving a vehicle that is longer, wider and taller than the one we have now. Can you offer me any insight?"

Joe: You're on the right course with your retirement plans. Both of you are acquainted with the RV lifestyle. You know how to use and enjoy an RV. Most importantly, you also recognize that a larger RV might be better suited for your extended travels.

Unfortunately, selecting an RV usually involves a compromise between mobility and living accommodations. A smaller rig allows you to travel narrow roads and to squeeze into tight campsites. It may also offer less wind resistance and better fuel economy. A larger RV, on the other hand, has room for the additional clothes, household items and those personal articles that convert your RV into a home away from home. A larger RV, obviously, has the room to provide more living comfort and convenience.

I can identify with your reluctance to move to a bigger RV. Our first rig was a 13-foot trailer. It was seven feet wide and almost eight feet high. The tow vehicle was a mid-size station wagon. Even though this towing combination was relatively short, I wondered if I would be comfortable driving it. My confidence zoomed, however, after I learned how to negotiate a right turn without the trailer's wheel going up on the curb.

Vicki: When we moved to a 17-foot trailer pulled by a Suburban, Joe had no problem at all adjusting to its additional length and the eight-foot wide body. He also adapted very quickly to the larger coach on our 24-foot Class C motorhome. Then we discussed buying a large Class A motorhome. Large, to me, meant about 35 feet. Joe had 28 feet in mind. Big deal! He seemed to think that anything longer than 28 feet should be on railroad tracks. We compromised on 32 feet. I couldn't find enough stuff to fill all the storage space.

Joe: While Vicki was looking for more stuff, I found myself adjusting to the larger motorhome. Surprisingly, the additional length didn't bother me at all. The rear end eventually seemed to get where the front end had traveled. My problem was getting used to the wider driving compartment. The eight-foot width of the Class A coach was the same as the Class C but the driving compartment was wider. My driver's seat was now located closer to the center of the highway. And Vicki wasn't thrilled about being closer to cars parked along the side if the road. It took a couple hundred miles of driving before both of us were comfortable with the wider driving compartment.

Vicki: Recently, we had the opportunity to drive and evaluate the livability of a 35-foot, motorhome. It was a 102-inch, wide-body model. Joe, once again, dragged his feet about driving a larger rig. He pointed out that with a car in tow our overall length would be 53 feet. And he wasn't so sure about the additional six inches of width, either. I mentioned it was only another 3 inches on either side but he pointed out that he was as close to oncoming traffic as he intended to get. When I volunteered to ride six inches closer to the curb, he shook his head, climbed into the driver's seat and started the engine.

Joe: Once again the additional length was no problem. I was amazed, though, at how easily I adapted to the extra width. I won't kid you; some narrow lanes did make me grip the steering wheel a little tighter and Vicki did jump one time when a street sign kissed the side-view mirror outside her window. But, all in all, I had little difficulty in adjusting to the additional width.

The point of all this is that you, like me and thousands of others, will probably adapt very quickly to driving a larger RV.

You might explain your concerns about driving a large motorhome to the salespeople. I'm sure they will be happy to provide you the opportunity to drive one while they give you some pointers to make you more comfortable. They might even be able to point you in the direction of a professional RV driving instructor.

If you still have doubts, rent a motorhome similar in size to the one you are considering. Take it out for a long weekend. Practice maneuvering in an empty parking lot. Drive it around town, on the open highway and in traffic. That should give you a pretty good idea of how easily you'll adapt to driving a larger RV.

In any case, don't give up your dream. Do see this great country of ours and, no matter what the size, do it in an RV.

A plastic turkey baster will make it easier for you to add distilled water to batteries located in hard to reach places.

Diesel Or Gasoline?

The question of whether to get a diesel or a gasoline powered RV has provided fuel for many campfire discussions. Some RVs, because of their weight, can only be moved by a diesel engine. Manufacturers of large motorhomes, for example, may build their coaches on diesel equipped truck chassis' and not offer a gasoline alternative. The manufacturers of gasoline-powered pickup trucks place a limit on the amount of weight their products can carry and tow. When the weight of the trailer exceeds that limit, the RVer usually has no choice but to buy a diesel-equipped truck.

There are motorhome and towing combinations, however, that offer a choice of gasoline or diesel engines. If you are seriously considering buying a diesel-powered RV, you should become familiar with the differences in the fuel, maintenance and operating characteristics of the diesel-equipped vehicle.

. Here are some points to consider when deciding between gasoline and diesel-equipped vehicles.

A diesel engine adds to the vehicle's purchase price, $3,500 or more for a pickup truck and $20,000 or more for a motorhome. As a result, the resale price of the diesel rig will usually be higher than the gasoline-powered RV.

A diesel has fewer moving parts and fewer electronics so it has less maintenance, repair and breakdowns. When they do occur, though, diesel repair and maintenance visits are generally more expensive than those for gasoline-equipped RVs.

The diesel engine will reportedly provide more than 300,000 miles of use before requiring serious engine work.

The gasoline engine, on the other hand, is usually due for overhaul at about 125,000 miles. Diesel engines, when located near the driver's compartment, are noisier than gasoline engines. The rear-engine diesel-pusher motorhome, however, removes the noise from the driver's compartment to the rear of the vehicle. The odor of diesel exhaust is objectionable to many. Diesel fuel is less volatile than gasoline. The diesel fueling process, though, can be messy.

We had a unique opportunity to compare two similar motorhomes, one with a gasoline engine and the other a diesel, under identical circumstances.

We once borrowed a gasoline powered, 36-foot motorhome for a 10,000 mile, three month speaking tour. The trip began the first of January in Southern California. We drove across the southern United States to Florida, traveled up the eastern seaboard to North Carolina, crossed the Appalachian Mountains to Missouri and returned to California by way of Northern Arizona.

We carried about 2,500 pounds of cargo and passengers and towed a 2,500 pound car. The driving and living conditions included rain, snow, ice, wind and temperatures that ranged from seventeen to ninety degrees. Elevations ranged from below sea level to above 5,000 feet. Our route took us through congested city traffic, along open interstates and across, hills, mountains and deserts.

The big block, V-8, gasoline engine performed considerably better than we had anticipated. It cruised along level and slightly rolling terrain at 60 to 65 miles per hour.

We were especially surprised at the drive train's ability to move that heavy RV across the mountains. The four speed automatic transmission dropped into third gear on grades of any consequence but hill climbing speed rarely dropped below 45 mph. Second gear was used only to prevent lugging the engine when uphill traffic slowed us down.

Fuel mileage for the trip averaged seven miles per gallon. We purchased all our gasoline at Flying J Travel Plazas. They have convenient RV fuel islands and their fuel prices are usually competitive for the area.

The next year our borrowed motorhome was a 37-foot diesel pusher. Again, we carried about 2,500 pounds of cargo and towed a 2,500 pound car. We followed essentially the same 10,000 mile route and encountered driving conditions similar to the previous year.

The turbo-powered 5.9 diesel responded faster than I had anticipated. It may have been a little slower than the gasoline engine during initial acceleration but it got up to cruising speed very quickly.

The drive train included a six speed transmission. Fifth and sixth gears were both overdrive gears. Cruising speed was an effortless 65 mph. Hills occasionally dropped the transmission into fifth gear and the tops of some mountain grades were reached in fourth. It was not unusual for us to pass gasoline-powered RVs on steeper grades.

The motorhome came equipped with an exhaust brake. Most downhill roads required only an occasional touch of the air brakes to maintain a safe and comfortable speed.

Fuel mileage for the diesel averaged 9.5 mile per gallon.

Our seat of the pants assessment of performance was that both vehicles accomplished the job quite satisfactorily. The diesel had a slight edge when climbing steep grades but the gasoline engine did not have any problems.

The diesel consumed less fuel and, in most states, the cost of diesel fuel was less than gasoline.

The diesel's fuel economy, however, was offset by the higher cost of oil and filter changes. We had the oil and filters changed according to the manufacturer's recommendations for heavy duty service. Both vehicles were serviced by the same RV dealers. The diesel's lubrication bill came to about three times that of the gasoline-powered rig. When we totaled up the cost of fuel, oil and filters for the 10,000 mile trip, the cost per mile was nearly the same for both rigs.

Based upon our observations, here is what we would suggest:

If you are only going to be using your RV for weekend trips and periodic two-to-three week vacations; if you will only take an occasional cross country trip; if you think you will put less than 100,000 miles on your rig over the next ten years; a less expensive, gasoline-powered rig might do the job very nicely for you.

On the other hand, if you are going to be moving heavy loads for long distances and will put a lot of miles on your rig, we would suggest you seriously consider the durability of a diesel engine. Its higher purchase price will probably be offset by its longevity, lower repair costs and higher resale value.

Whichever you choose, your decision will provide plenty of fuel for those campfire discussions.

You won't lose your fuel filler cap if you put hook and loop tape on your fuel filler cap and the inside of the fuel filler door. Just hang the cap on the fuel filler door.

Accessories, Gadgets, Necessities

"It's time to buy another RV. We know what type and size we want but are having trouble deciding what options, add-ons and accessories to get. Would you mind telling us which you would want on your next RV?"

Joe: Slowly but surely a lot of yesterday's optional accessories and gadgets have become, for us, today's necessities. Here are a few we would not want to do without:

Windshield sunscreens - These screens reduce the amount of sun (and heat) that radiates through the windshield. And, while they allow us to see what's going on outside, they prevent passerbys from seeing into our living area. We chose the type that mount on the inside of the windshield. They are easy to put up and take down, stay dry when it rains and rarely need cleaning.

Awnings all around - Glass can radiate an amazing amount of heat into an RV. The large awning on our curb-side wall and the awnings over each of our windows keep this from happening.

Dual-pane windows - There must be a rule that requires commercial campgrounds to be located within a half mile of a busy railroad track and/or under the landing approach of an airport. Dual-pane windows do an excellent job of minimizing and sometimes eliminating these sleep disrupters. By the way, dual-pane windows do an outstanding job of insulating against outside temperatures. We have come to really appreciate them when we are camping in cold weather.

Air conditioners - We are fresh-air fiends. Our RV was selected because it has lots of windows. They open wide and provide plenty of cross ventilation. There are plenty of occasions, however, when the windows get shut and the air conditioner(s) are turned on. We would never leave home without them.

Inverter - What a wonderful invention. It takes 12-volt battery power and turns it into 120-volt household electricity. We used to make coffee in a range-top percolator when we did not have an electrical hookup. Oh, we could have fired up the generator but, at that hour of the morning, we did not think our neighbors would appreciate the noise nor the smell of the exhaust. Now, with the inverter, we can still use our electric coffee maker. The inverter also makes it possible for us to operate electric appliances, like the computer, while we are driving down the road.

Generator - Most RV air conditioners require about 2,000 watts of 120-volt, AC electrical power. That's more than can be supplied by a couple of deep-cycle batteries and an inverter. So, if you want to operate your RV's air conditioner when you don't have an electrical hookup, you're going to need a generator. Generators come in a variety of sizes and capabilities. If you're going to spend the money for a generator, get one that provides sufficient wattage to operate one or both of your air-conditioners. Figure 2,000 watts for each roof air conditioner. Add another 1,500 watts if you want to operate a microwave or hair dryer while the air conditioner is running. Throw in another 500 to 1,000 watts for good measure and you're looking at a 6,500 watt generator.

Gas/electric water heater - An RV's gas water heater is a heavy consumer of propane. It burns propane for a half hour or longer to heat the initial tank of water. The flame then periodically roars to life throughout the day and night to maintain the water's temperature setting. An optional, built-in electric heating element saves propane and silently maintains the water temperature whenever you have an electrical hookup. We added an after-market 120-volt AC heating element to the propane water heater of our previous RV. It worked great.

Roof-vent covers - Opening a roof vent allows heat, condensation and cooking odors to escape the confines of an RV. Opening a roof vent when it's raining, though, results in a wet floor. Adding a roof vent cover permits you to open the roof vent when it's raining, windy and even while you're driving down the road.

High-powered, roof-vent fan - Capable of a variety of speeds, these fans will quickly remove hot air through the roof vent and/or draw cool air in through the windows. On warm, humid nights, rather than run the air conditioner, we open the bedroom windows an inch or two, close all the other RV windows and turn on the roof-vent fan. The air drawn through the bedroom windows feels like a soft, cool breeze. During the winter, we minimize condensation by opening a window (a quarter-inch or so) at each end of our rig and operating the kitchen roof-vent fan at a slow speed.

Portable electric heater - Once your RV's propane-fired furnace has warmed up the interior of your RV, a small electric heater will keep things cozy for a long time. Since the RV's forced-air furnace is one of the heaviest consumers of propane, you'll also appreciate the added benefit of not having to refill your tanks too often.

Microwave/convection oven. Quick meal preparation and cool operation. The convection oven will do just about anything a gas oven will do, except heat up the interior of the RV. A gas oven is nice, though, when you don't have electric hookups and don't want to disturb the peace and quiet with your generator.

Clothes washer/dryer - We have been washing our clothes in laundromats and campground laundry rooms for over 35 years. Never saw the need and did not want to sacrifice the space for a washer in our RV. Today, if we did not spend months at a time traveling in our motorhome, we still would not choose to have a washer/dryer. But, living in our rig as we do, we appreciate the convenience of doing laundry in our RV almost as much as the luxury of being able to shower in it.

Booth dinette - Originally, our motorhome came equipped with a dining table and free-standing chairs. The arrangement really looked spacious. And the chairs were certainly easy to get in and out of. But, we missed the huge storage drawers found under the seats of a booth dinette and the comfort of curling up on a cushion while working or playing at the table. So, we gave the folks at the factory a heart attack and asked them to take out the chairs and put in booth seats.

Larger horsepower engine - This was an expensive option but we would do it again. We actually manage to pass other RVs while going uphill. Fuel mileage may be slightly less than with the smaller engine, but then it was not fuel mileage we were concerned about when climbing steep mountain grades in our previous motorhome.

Exhaust brake - Diesel powered vehicles do not slow down a whole lot when you take your foot off the accelerator. That means using the brakes to control your downhill speed. An exhaust brake changes all that. Take your foot off the accelerator and the engine really slows the vehicle down. There are actually occasions when we have to press slightly on the accelerator to get down a grade.

Roll out storage trays - At first glance their presence appears to take away storage space from the exterior storage bays. But the ability to open a bay and pull out its contents on a drawer-like shelf allows you to make more effective use of what used to be almost inaccessible space.

Hydraulic, electric or airbag leveling system - A real back saver. But don't throw away your lumber collection. There will be times when even the RV's leveling system cannot overcome the slope of a substandard campsite and you will have to drive your wheels up on the old-fashion leveling boards.

Water filter - America's water is not getting any purer. A sediment filter outside the RV screens out silt, bugs and loose debris that makes its way into the various water systems you connect to (we've found all of them in our sediment filter). A carbon filter located after the sediment filter (inside or outside the RV) will remove strange tastes and odors from the water.

You really don't need any of this stuff to enjoy RVing. We didn't have any of it when we bought our first or even our second RV. Somehow, as you go down the road, accessories and gadgets accumulate and the next thing you know ... they become necessities.

Clothes Washer/Dryer

"In a previous column you discussed the pros and cons of having a clothes washer/dryer in your RV. You said that you would consider installing one in a future RV if you had the space. Did you get a washer/dryer in your new RV? How do you like it?"

Joe: For the benefit of those who did not read that column and for those who are considering a washer/dryer in their rig, we will start at the beginning.

Clothes washing machines and dryers are offered as an option in many of today's RVs. You can also buy and install them as an after-market product.

The owners of some larger RVs install apartment-size stack washers and dryers. Most RVers, however, prefer the smaller, front-loading, combination washer/dryers.

There are two types of combination washer/dryers; vented and non-vented.

Vented machines, during the drying process, take room air, heat it, tumble it through the clothes and exhaust it to the outside. This means a hole has to be made in the wall of the RV for the exhaust vent.

Non-vented machines heat air inside the drum and tumble it through the clothes. This creates steam within the drum. Cold water is then used to cool the outside of the drum. This condenses the steam to water which is pumped into the RV's drain and holding tank.

Depending upon the size of the machine, you can put from 7 to 10 pounds of clothes in a single wash load. This is about one-third to one-half of what will fit in your full size washing machine at home.

The wash cycle, depending upon the type and size of the load, can take anywhere from 30 to 45 minutes. The drying cycle takes 60 to 90 minutes. Heavy items such as towels, jeans and sweatshirts may take even more time. The washer/dryers require 115 volts of AC electricity and draw about 13 amps while operating. A 30-amp campground hookup will provide the necessary electrical power but that leaves only 17 amps to meet the rest of the RV's needs. Keep in mind that operating your high amperage microwave, space heater or hair dryer while the washer/dryer is working could overload a 30-amp circuit.

It takes 16 to 20 gallons of water (more, in some cases) to wash a load of clothes. Non-vented machines will use an additional 3 - 5 gallons of water during the drying cycle.

It is possible to operate the washer/dryer by using the RV's generator for power and relying upon its fresh-water and holding tanks but that would put a serious dent in your rig's self-containment capacities. If you do use the washer/dryer this way, be sure to keep an eye on your monitor panel. The last thing you want to do is overflow your holding tank.

Vicki: Last year, after it had accumulated over 100,000 miles, we traded in our 10-year old, 32- foot motorhome on a 36-foot diesel pusher. Once again, while we were shopping, Joe asked if I wanted a washer/dryer. Once again, I replied that if it meant sacrificing valuable interior storage space, I would rather continue using the campground laundry rooms.

As it turned out, the motorhome we selected had plenty of storage space. It also had a pre-plumbed cabinet that could accommodate a washer/dryer. We traveled and lived in that motorhome for the first three months without a washer/dryer. During that time the washer/dryer cabinet was left empty to see if we could get along without that storage space. We decided to get the washer/dryer.

We chose a vented unit. It was installed with a drain pan underneath that could catch and drain off any water that might leak or spill.

The washer/dryer does a great job. I put in dirty clothes and take out clean, dry clothes. Works every time.

I have found that I can keep ahead of our laundry by washing one load of clothes every day or so. I usually use campground laundry rooms to wash bedsheets, heavy towels and jeans because their machines are faster,.

Since most of the campgrounds we stay in have only 30-amp hookups, I have gotten into the habit of waiting until after dinner to turn on the washer. That way I am not using the washer, microwave and electric coffee pot simultaneously. I can operate the washer anytime, though, when we have 50-amp hookups.

Would I recommend having a washer/dryer in an RV. Here comes one of those "it depends" answers. We travel and live in our RV for months at a time. It is literally our home on wheels. Having a washer on board provides the same convenience as our washing machine at home. If we only used our RV a couple weekends a month and for an occasional two-to-three week vacation I don't know if I could justify the expense of a washer/dryer. On the other hand, if my husband can watch sports events on satellite TV, and keep track of himself with a ground positioning satellite system, why shoudn't I be able to wash his socks in a washer/dryer?

RV Washer/Dryer And Bleach

"Do you use bleach in your RV's washing machine? What do you do about hair coloring or peroxide? Will these chemicals hurt the plumbing or holding tank? And, was it you who said not to use anti-bacterial soap?"

Vicki: Wow! A bunch of real life questions. I love it. Yes, I do use bleach in my washing machine. Like you, I wondered if it would damage the holding tank or its valves. Then I thought about it and realized, "wait a minute -- if I can't use this machine the way it was intended, what good is it? If I shouldn't use bleach, why does the manufacturer have a bleach dispenser on the machine?"

I also color my hair in the RV. After applying the coloring, rather than taking a chance on staining our shower walls, I rinse the coloring out of my hair in our stainless steel kitchen sink. Then I jump into the shower to shampoo, etc.

It must have been someone else who told you not to use anti-bacterial soaps. We do use them, especially after handling the sewer hose.

We bought our motorhome to live in. If our living in it damages the holding tank valves or anything else, we'll just have to replace them.

Measuring Up

"During your "10 Tips For Choosing An RV" seminar, Vicki tells the audience to try an RV on for size to see if it fits. Do you have any other tips for evaluating the livability of an RV?"

One of the best tools to help you select an RV is a tape measure. Here are some places you might want to measure:

Outside storage bays essentially take the place of your attic or garage. Will there be room for your golf clubs, fishing gear, outside furniture, barbecue, tools, spare parts, leveling blocks and hookup equipment? Compare the dimensions of these larger items to the sizes of the outside storage bays.

Windows provide visibility, ventilation and a sense of interior spaciousness. If you're a fresh air fiend, windows that open wide and provide plenty of cross ventilation will be important to you.

Kitchen counter tops can be important if you plan to do much cooking. It's not unusual to see an RV come equipped with a large side-by-side refrigerator, ice-maker, propane oven, microwave/convection oven, pull-out pantry, double sink and dining accommodations for six people. But that same rig may have little or no counter space on which to prepare a meal or stack dirty dishes.

Kitchen sinks should be deep enough to wash your largest pot. We've noticed that the sinks in some RVs take up more counter top area than in others, yet their usable interior dimensions are no larger.

Refrigerator interiors generally seem pretty satisfactory. Measure to be sure they will be able to carry one-quart containers of milk, fat jars of pickles and tall bottles of salad dressing. Or plan on transferring these items to smaller containers.

Does the side-by-side refrigerator offer the same (or more) practical carrying capacity as the standard over-and-under refrigerator? Would you rather have the extra freezer capacity of a side-by-side refrigerator or would you prefer the slide-out pantry that may accompany a standard refrigerator?

Slideout pantry. It may look big but will it accommodate boxes of cold cereal and bags of potato chips or just small sizes of canned goods?

Interior cabinets will be used to store a variety of items. Will your coffee pot, toaster, crockpot, pressure cooker, electric skillet, pots, pans, lids, serving bowls, dishes, cups and glasses fit into the available storage cabinets?

Our tape measure revealed that the height of the cabinets in one RV wouldn't accommodate our coffee pot in an upright position nor would the depth permit our dinner plates to lay flat.

We use decent sized transparent plastic boxes to store things in overhead cabinets. It is important to us that the cabinets are large enough to accommodate them.

Bench seat dinettes are preferred by many RVers because of the storage underneath and because they can be converted into a guest bed. Two people should sit down on each side to try it on for elbow room. And they should sit across from one another to see if their knees touch (this may be desirable for some).

Your tape measure will also reveal how long the guest bed is and how much accessible storage is underneath.

Waste basket. Where does the waste basket go? We discovered a long time ago that the little wire contraption attached to the cupboard door under the sink wouldn't hold the volume nor support the weight of our trash. We use a standard, house-size waste basket and we need a place to put it. Measure your waste basket and then identify a logical location where it willl fit.

Mattresses. Have you ever tried putting form fitting sheets on an RV mattress? That's when you find out that not all RV mattresses have the same dimensions as those in your house.

Here are the standard mattress sizes according to a mattress manufacturer:

California King	72" by 84"
Eastern King	76" by 80"
Queen	60" by 80"
Full	53" by 74"
Twin	38" by 74"

There's nothing wrong with a mattress that isn't a standard size, but you do want to make an informed decision.

Clothes closets. It doesn't make sense to hang your clothes neatly in a closet only to have the bottom six inches laying rumpled on the closet floor.

At home, measure the shoulder width of the widest garment you expect to hang in your RV's clothes closet. Next, measure from the top of that clothes rod to the bottom of the longest item of clothing you expect to hang in your RV's closet. Then, measure from the top of your clothes rod to the bottom of the shirts and slacks you have on hangers.

Use these measurements to determine if the RV's clothes closets and shirt lockers will accommodate the clothes you wish to take.

Drawers. Most drawer items will fit one way or the other but some RVs have more drawers with better dimensions.

Open every drawer. You'd be surprised at how short some of them can be. Compare the number and size of the drawers in the kitchen, bedroom and bathroom of every prospective rig.

Shower. Surprise, surprise! Take your shoes off and step into the shower. Go through the motions of taking a shower and washing your hair. Can you accomplish this without bruising your knuckles on the ceiling or getting wrapped up in the shower curtain? Be reasonable, most RV showers won't compare to the one you have at home, but do measure and compare the various showers available for the type and size rig you are looking at.

Towel holders If the towel holders that come with the RV are insufficient or too small, you can install your own. But where? Measure the available wall or door space.

Medicine chest. Is the medicine chest deep enough and its shelves high enough to accommodate the items you plan to put in it?

Some folks install a short barrier on each medicine chest shelf to prevent the contents from spilling out after a day on the road. Is the medicine chest you're looking at deep enough for you to do the same?

Couch. "Sleeps two." At least that's what the brochure claims. Does it mean two adults or two children? Convert the couch into a bed. Lie down on both sides. Is it comfortable? A six-foot person would appreciate a bed that is at least 74 inches long.

Is there storage underneath the couch? How is it accessed? What are the dimensions?

Fresh water tank and holding tanks. Sometimes the capacity of a water tank or holding tank is unknown or in question. Determine the tank's number of cubic inches by multiplying length by width by height. Now divide the tank's cubic inches by 231. This should tell you the approximate number of gallons the tank will hold.

That tape measure will also come in handy for measuring exterior dimensions, wheel base, rear overhang, ground clearance, and other important exterior items.

Next time you go looking at RVs take your tape measure. It will literally tell you if an RV is going to measure up to your expectations.

Spiders are attracted to the scent of propane. They build webs in the small orifices that control the flow of propane to your gas appliances. This interferes with their proper operation. When you put your RV into storage, place a sock containing a few mothballs inside the exterior access doors of the water heater and refrigerator. This will prevent the spiders from taking up residence. Be sure to remove the sock before you fire up the appliance.

Identify keys by painting them with colored fingernail polish. You could also paint the corresponding lock with the same color.

Our RV

"What kind of RV do you have? "

Vicki: We have owned a variety of RVs over the past 35 years. As young newlyweds we used to borrow an umbrella tent for weekend getaways. When our first child arrived we purchased a very used, 13-foot vacation trailer.

A few years later, we were towing a 17-foot trailer. It was perfect for weekends and our two to three week vacations. One year, our family of five spent five months touring the United States in that trailer.

Next came a 24-foot Class C motorhome. Its bunk beds gave each of our teenagers a space to call their own. That motorhome made a number of cross-country trips and took us on our first Alaska adventure.

With the kids grown and gone, we purchased a 32-foot Class A motorhome powered by a gasoline engine. What a great touring machine that was. It took us from Nova Scotia to Puerto Vallarta and from Miami Beach to Fairbanks. We went out on the road for two to three months at a time, returned home for a month or two and then hit the highways for another couple of months. We had become extended RV travelers.

When the Class A's speedometer approached 100,000 miles we realized it was time to get a new RV that would complement our extended traveling lifestyle.

We took our own advice. We examined our RV lifestyle and determined our interests, needs and budget. Then we started searching for the "perfect" RV.

We needed another touring machine. Last year we spent eight months on the road and put over 20,000 miles on our rig. Our RV is our home (and office) away from home. We take a lot of stuff with us to complement our seminar and writing business. Obviously, we needed a rig designed and built to carry heavy loads over long distances for sustained periods of time.

We wanted a condo on wheels. Living amenities are important when you spend a lot of time actually living in an RV. What may amount to a minor inconvenience (a small bathroom for example) during a two-week vacation can become a serious aggravation after a couple of months on the road. We needed a rig built to withstand the constant wear and tear of full-time living. Something comfortable yet functional and durable.

Joe: Finally, after two years of shopping, we found it. A 36-foot, wide-body, diesel-powered, class-A motorhome. It more than satisfies our interests and needs. It's our dream machine.

Its 325 horsepower engine and six-speed transmission flattens out mountains and delivers 8 miles to the gallon.

Air bag suspension provides a smooth, quiet ride and levels the motorhome in the campground.

Large air brakes, assisted by an engine-exhaust brake, take all the excitement out of those long downhill runs with a car in tow.

The cargo-carrying capacity is more than adequate. Fully loaded for travel and carrying 1,000 pounds of books and seminar materials we still have 1,500 pounds of cargo carrying capacity.

Self-contained camping is a snap with a 100 gallon fresh-water tank, 134 gallons of waste water capacity and a 42 gallon propane tank. When we don't want to run our diesel generator we can utilize the two 8D coach batteries and 2,000 watt inverter.

A crowned, one-piece, fiberglass roof sheds rain as fast as it falls.

R11 fiberglass in the roof, 1 1/2 inch polystyrene in the floors and walls and dual-paned windows insulate the interior from outside temperatures and noise.

Awnings on the curbside wall and above all the windows keep out the direct rays of the sun.

Air conditioning units and high-volume roof-vent fans cool the interior during our summer circuit.

The fully equipped kitchen has adequate counter space and the usual appliances. We especially appreciate the gas/electric water heater and the microwave/convection oven.

We added a washer/dryer. Vicki loves it but she also uses the campground laundry room. She says "That's where you meet people and find out what's down the road."

Hanging locker space, drawers and cupboards swallow up all the clothes we carry.

Heating duct outlets built into the cabinetry can be aimed to heat the surface of the floor.

Plumbing enclosed in a heated compartment is protected from the freezing temperatures we encounter during our winter show circuit.

No, we did not feel the need for a slideout room. Yes, we preferred the storage and versatility of a bench seat dinette. No, we definitely did not want a bigger RV.

It took a while but, once again, we managed to find an RV that satisfies our interests and needs. We love it. Now, all we have to do . . . is pay for it!

Dinghy Towing

"We will be trading in our 24-foot Class C motorhome on a 34-foot Class A motorhome. We never felt the need to tow a car behind our 24 footer. We used the motorhome for transportation while camping. Will the longer motorhome require us to tow a small car? Which towing method is easiest?"

Joe: To tow or not to tow, that is the question. The answer is... it all depends.

We enjoyed a 24-foot Class C motorhome for many years. Like you, we never felt the need for an auxiliary transportation vehicle.

That motorhome went just about anywhere a car could go. It fit very nicely into two tandem parking spaces at supermarkets and shopping centers. Its relatively short wheelbase allowed us to maneuver in and out of the parking lots of some very nice restaurants. It took us to places like Alaska, Mexico and the Canadian Maritime Provinces. We only had to pay for one vehicle when we went through toll booths or boarded a ferry. On the few occasions when we felt the need for a car; we discovered that car rental agencies would deliver to campgrounds.

Vicki: And then our RV lifestyle changed. Among other things, we found ourselves staying in one place for longer than two or three days at a time. Disconnecting from and reconnecting to campground hookups every time we wanted to go to the store or a restaurant was a real bother. When we bought a 32-foot Class A motorhome, we started towing a car.

Learning how to hitch up the car took us back to the days when we learned how to hitch up a travel trailer. I would drive the car while Joe held the tow bar and directed me to just the right position for connecting the tow bar to the hitchball. At first there was much yelling, waving of arms, rolling of eyeballs and knashing of teeth. And you should have seen and heard Joe.

But, just as we did with the trailer, we developed a smooth, coordinated system of hitching up the car. By the way, we found that the best place to unhitch the car was in the campground-registration parking area. It is usually level and the motorhome and car are aligned so the towbar is not binding against the hitchball. While I go in to register, Joe unhitches the car. Having the vehicles separate also makes it easier to maneuver through the campground and into our campsite.

Our present RV lifestyle has us working on the road for two to four months at a time. It is a rare occasion when our 36-foot motorhome goes down the road without our car in tow.

I am sure you will appreciate the convenience of having a transportation vehicle if your RV lifestyle includes staying in one place for longer than a few days at a time.

Joe: There are three methods of towing a car. You can load the car onto a trailer, put its drive wheels on a tow-dolly or tow the car with all four wheels on the ground. Towing with all four wheels down is the easiest and most convenient method.

Not all cars are towable, however. The drive train of many vehicles equipped with automatic transmissions and/or front wheel drive can be damaged if they are towed with all four wheels on the ground.

If that is the case with your car, there are after-market products available (transmission lubrication pumps, transmission uncouplers and drive-wheel lockout devices) that may overcome this obstacle. Otherwise you may have no choice but to tow with a trailer or tow dolly.

For simplicity, we would recommend that you get a car that can be towed with all four wheels on the ground. Saturn, for example, brags in writing that all their late-model cars can be towed with all four wheels down. Hitch the car to the motorhome, put the car's transmission in neutral, turn the key to accessory and go. It's that simple.

Vicki: Today, you don't have to go through the "learning-how" agonies of hitching up that we once did. Get a telescoping, self-adjusting tow bar like Blue Ox's Aladdin tow bar. The tow bar remains permanently attached to the motorhome's hitch receiver. Its telescoping arms fold snug against the rear bumper when not towing. When it's time to tow, all you have to do is position the car "close enough" to the motorhome. The towbar arms telescope to the car's connection tabs. When you drive the motorhome forward, the tow-bar arms automatically lock into place.

This combination makes hitching and unhitching a very easy, one-person operation.

Joe: Check with the manufacturer of your motorhome to be sure the weight of your car will not cause you to exceed the motorhome's gross combined weight rating.

Be sure you read the small print in your motorhome's literature. You may find that, while the motorhome may be rated to tow up to 5,000 pounds, its brakes are only rated to safely stop a towed vehicle of less than 1,500 pounds. You may need to equip your car with a braking system that will activate the car's brakes in conjunction with the motorhome's.

Vicki: Towing a car behind a big motorhome can be simple, easy and a real convenience. Especially if the hitching and unhitching is a one-person process (and guess who that one person is? Guess who goes outside to hook up the car and who gets to stay inside when it is raining? Yes!! I love it!).

When backing a trailer, place your hand at the bottom of the steering wheel. Move the bottom of the steering wheel in the direction you want the rear of the trailer to move.

Dinghy Protection

" Do you use a cover over the front of your car to keep dirt and gravel from hurting it while towing? Have you ever used those shields that ride in front of the car?"

Joe: When we first began towing a car we bought one of those fiberglass shields and a padded, vinyl windshield cover. Never experienced any damage to the windshield or front of the car. Although, after a few years, I did notice rub marks wearing into the paint above the windshield. Apparently this was caused by the cover moving slightly while we traveled down the road. Occasionally, I also noticed little pieces of road tar stuck on the top of the hood. They brushed off quite easily, however.

There was the question of what to do with the shield once we arrived at our destination. I usually stowed it under the motorhome and hoped the wind wouldn't blow it away. Actually, I felt that putting on and taking off the shield and windshield cover was a bother.

After we installed some large mud flaps behind the rear wheels of the motorhome, we stopped using the fiberglass shield. Later we stopped using the vinyl windshield cover. After ten years and over 100,000 towing miles we never experienced any damage to the front of that car.

Last summer we purchased a new car for towing. We don't use a car cover nor do we use a shield. The only protection for that car are the mud flaps behind the motorhome's rear tires and a solid, heavy mud flap the width of the rear bumper. It almost touches the ground.

So far, we have towed that car 10,000 miles, driven it 2,500 miles and not experienced any damage.

Preparing For Your RV's Arrival

"After two years of research we have purchased our first RV, a motorhome. It will be a while before we take delivery. Is there anything we should do to prepare for its arrival?"

Joe: Begin by locating a place to store it. The average RV spends more time in storage than on the road. You want a storage spot that is secure, convenient and easy to get in and out of.

The ideal storage location is inside a garage or barn on your property. Not only would it be convenient, it would also protect your RV from thieves, vandals and the elements.

Second choice might be in the rear or side yard of your home. You will want to check first to see if there are any local ordinances or homeowner association rules that prohibit RVs from being parked on your property or in front of your house.

Some RVers, who store their rigs on their property, install a concrete pad with water, electricity and sewer connections. A reasonably level spot, however, is all you really need. Having a 20-amp electrical outlet and water spigot nearby would be an added bonus.

You may decide that a professional storage facility is your best choice. Look for one that is fenced and perhaps even has a security guard. Be sure it is conveniently located and offers easy entry and exit. You do not want to go through a lot of bother every time you drop off or pick up your rig.

With any luck, the storage lot will have a dump station and/or wash rack; many do.

Filling your fuel tank before putting your RV into storage will minimize the formation of condensation and resultant water problems inside the tank. Check out the fuel stations in your area. Look for one that offers convenient RV access. Be careful of the overhead clearance. You do not want to peel off your roof air-conditioning unit as you approach the pumps.

Keep in mind that a busy fuel station will have fresher fuel. This is especially important if you have a diesel engine. Try to locate a station that has an accessible air hose so you can keep your tires at the appropriate pressure. By the way, do not rely on the accuracy of the gauge on the end of the air hose. Invest in a good tire pressure gauge.

Look for a place to refill your propane tank(s). This could be an RV dealership, RV accessory store or a service station. Propane cylinders on trailers can be removed and transported in a truck or car to be refilled. The propane tanks on motorhomes, however, are permanently mounted to the frame. The motorhome, therefore, must be able to get fairly close to the propane filling pump.

Try to locate a disposal station that is reasonably close to your home. Most RVers try to dump their holding tanks at the campground before heading for home. Once in a while, though, you'll have need for a dump station close to home. Again, RV dealerships, RV accessory stores or service stations may offer a place to dispose of your waste water. Other places to check for disposal stations would be nearby roadside rest areas, campgrounds and even the local waste-water treatment plant.

Some RVers have discovered they are able to empty their holding tanks into their home's sewer system. Many do this by connecting the RV sewer hose to a cleanout access plug in their house's sewer line. Be sure you ask a plumber's advice before you try to do the same.

Locate a nearby lube and oil-change shop. Check the garage's door clearances and look for hazards that may not seem obvious. One RVer we know had the side of his rig blistered by a space heater attached to the ceiling of a lube garage. Don't rule out a business, though, just because your RV won't fit through the door. Some can accomplish the job outside. If the facility looks like it can handle your rig, ask if they work on RVs. You could also ask if they will use the oil and filters you provide.

Now is the time to locate an RV repair and maintenance facility. The RV dealership where you purchased your RV may be a logical choice. Look for one that has experience with your type and make of rig. Be sure they are authorized to perform any warranty work you may have done on your RV. Ask if they can work on the coach, chassis, engine and transmission of your vehicle. You may have to line up more than one repair facility.

With any luck, you will be able to wash your rig in your driveway or on the street in front of your house. Otherwise, you should locate a self-service car wash that will accommodate an RV (not all do). Look around. Some have catwalks that make it easy for you to wash your roof. The really good ones will offer high pressure and steam cleaning hoses.

Chances are you'll spend a few hundred dollars accessorizing that new RV during the first year of ownership. Locate an RV accessory store that is well stocked and offers installation at a reasonable price. Ask them to notify you of their sales by putting you on their mailing list. Pick up a copy of their catalog. You'll soon refer to it as your RV "wish book."

Knowing the location of all these services and facilities will save you a lot of time and frustration. Don't overlook the obvious. Begin your search with the dealer who sold you your RV. Chances are your dealer offers a good number of the services you want or need.

Vicki: As soon as you take delivery of your RV you will want to get acquainted with it. The best way to accomplish this is for you to thoroughly clean that rig, inside and out. This will give you a hands on, personal inspection of every inch of your RV. You will also know that any future dust and dirt you run across is yours. And that every dent and ding you discover occurred after you took possession.

Begin by emptying out and vacuuming out all the outside storage bays. Open every exterior access door (refrigerator, water heater, generator, etc.) and clean the interior of the compartment. This is your opportunity to look for loose screws, torn carpet and fluid leaks.

Wash the outside. Be sure to spray lots of water around everything that protrudes from the roof. Air conditioning units, antennas, vents and skylights should all be sealed to prevent any water from getting inside. Don't be bashful about wetting down the perimeter of the windows. They should also be water tight. Once you've soaked the outside of your RV, go inside and check for leaks.

Most RVers use a soft-bristled brush on a telescoping handle to wash the outside of their rig. Use a vehicle washing soap approved by the manufacturer of the RV.

Next, vacuum and clean all the interior closets, cupboards, cabinets and drawers. Look for any loose hinges, locks or hardware.

Pull out the drawers and vacuum the empty space behind and underneath them.

Open every interior access door (heater air inlet, plumbing access, fuse box) and carefully vacuum or clean the interior.

Notice the location of the wiring and plumbing while you are inside the cupboards and behind the drawers. You do not want to store anything where it can damage the pipes or wires.

Wipe down the woodwork with a wood cleaner and preservative. The one you use on your furniture at home should do the job very nicely.

Vacuum the upholstery. Lift the seat cushions (is there access to the space below?). Get under the couch (can this area be used for storage? Are there seatbelts here?).

Wash the windows. Search for signs of leaks. Check the locking hardware. Look for loose or damaged screens.

By this time, your RV is clean and ready for you to move in. You may also have discovered a few nooks and crannies that can be utilized for storage. Best of all, you will have gotten personally acquainted with every inch of your rig.

RV Packing Tips

Joe: A cardinal rule for packing an RV is "a place for everything and everything in its place."

You want to be sure the "place" for each thing is located where it travels well, makes sense and is easily accessible.

Ideally, every item you have in your RV will remain in its travel place except when you are using it.

Here are a few packing tips that may help you find a place for everything.

Things have a tendency to relocate themselves during travel. Try placing non-skid material on the bottom of cupboards to keep them from sliding around and breaking.

Partitions made of cardboard, masonite or wood will prevent tall items like a coffee pot from tipping over.

Another way to keep things from moving around is to keep them in containers - boxes, bins or bags

Cardboard boxes are inexpensive, lightweight, come in various sizes and can be cut to fit if necessary. Cover the outsides with self-sticking, vinyl shelf paper. This will reinforce the box and make it more attractive.

Transparent plastic storage boxes of various sizes can be packed in your house and carried to the RV. Kept in overhead lockers, you can see what's inside and pull them out like a drawer. At the end of the trip, the box can be brought into the house and unpacked.

Look for storage boxes designed to fit under beds. Chances are they will fit under your RV's couch. They can also be used in the hard-to-reach center section of your basement model storage lockers.

Ziplock bags and transparent plastic food containers are ideal for spill-proof, space-efficient, refrigerator storage. They also make efficient use of cupboard space.

Some folks transfer foods from their original king-size packages into smaller plastic containers. Others buy smaller size containers of food.

Vicki: Another observation about packing an RV is that the amount of stuff you take is directly proportional to the amount of storage space you you are able to locate or create.

You may be able to create more storage space by installing shelves and partitions inside cupboards. Make them adjustable to accommodate any changes you may want to make later.

Add shelves, drawers or cabinets to the bottom of the wardrobe closet where the space for full length clothes is not needed.

Place clothes hooks in corners or out of the way spots.

Install clothes-rod brackets at each end of your shower. A removable clothes rod can be placed in the shower to hang wet clothes or rain gear

The shower is also a handy place to keep your laundry bag. The bag can be moved temporarily while you shower. Laundry supplies can be kept in a laundry basket in an outside storage cabinet.

You'll want to pack things according to their priority. Pack the absolute necessities first. The things you think you need next and so on.

The kitchen will probably be the busiest area of your RV. Begin packing there first.

Put cooking and eating utensils where they make the most sense for convenient preparation and serving of meals.

Place some non-skid padding or terry-cloth toweling between Teflon pans to prevent scratching or rubbing of the Teflon coating. The same cushioning between nested pots and pans will minimize noise.

Locate food items where they will be readily accessible.

Dishwashing and kitchen cleaning materials should also be handy.

The bathroom is easy. You'll want everyday toiletries easily accessible. Each individual's toiletries can be packed in transparent plastic shoe boxes while at home, stored in the RV's bathroom cabinet during the trip and moved back to the home bathroom upon your return

Daily medicines should be up front or at eye level. Seldom used medications can be relegated to the harder to reach locations.

A plastic box to hold soap and shampoo while traveling should also be easy to reach when needed.

Towels and wash cloths can be hung on towelracks attached to the bathroom walls or door.

Most of today's RVs have a large storage space under the bed. The space is usually accessible by lifting the bed platform. This place is ideal for seldom used, large or bulky items like ironing boards and vacuum cleaners. Plastic storage boxes (with or without the lids) can make optimum use of this space.

Take only the clothes you'll need for that trip. Mix-and-match outfits will minimize the number of clothes you need.

Pack no more than seven to ten days worth of clothing. Plan on doing laundry that often.

You can save hanging locker space by taking wrinkle-resistant, foldable clothes.

Rolling, rather than folding, clothes sometimes takes less space.

Cold weather garb can be stored in an outside storage cabinets during warm weather. Summer clothes can be stored in the outside cabinet during cold weather.

Joe: Outside, begin packing the storage cabinets at the utility hookup cabinet. Leveling and hooking up the RV may take place as often as every day. You'll want the hookup and leveling equipment convenient and accessible.

Drinking water hose(s), water filter, pressure regulator and other water hookup items should be stowed in a clean location in or near the utility hookup cabinet..

Sewer hose(s) and connections, electrical adapters, TV cable and telephone cable should be stowed nearby but not so they can contaminate the drinking water equipment.

Store patio furniture and outdoor cooking equipment on the entry-door side of the RV. That's where you will be using them.

Large, strong, plastic boxes or tubs will provide maximum effective use of exterior space.

If you install a storage pod on the roof, carefully consider its location and orientation.

Ideally, the pod will be located so the weight of its cargo is above or in front of the rear axle.

Mounting it lengthwise, in line with the air conditioners, will minimize wind resistance while driving down the highway but increase the exposure to gusts of side winds.

Reserve the storage pod for lightweight items that only get occasional use. Heavy items will elevate the RV's center of gravity and you will want to minimize the weight of anything that has to be carried up and down the ladder.

Keep a length of rope available in one of the RV's exterior lockers. Use the rope to raise or lower your roof pod items. Old suitcases and dufflebags work well here.

Tools may be more accessible if kept in the trailer's tow vehicle or the motorhome's towed vehicle.

Vicki: You can minimize packing and unpacking your RV between trips by permanently storing as much as possible in the RV.

Equip the RV kitchen with its own cooking and eating utensils, appliances and non-perishable food items.

Equip the bathroom so each person has to bring only a minimum of personal toiletries and medications.

Keep your RV stocked so you only have to add perishable foods and a few items of clothing before getting on the road.

Lists are especially helpful. Joe and I maintain a list of the things we routinely pack in our RV before each trip.

We also make a list of special items we want to take for the upcoming trip. Perhaps an item we want to deliver to friends along the way or a piece of camping gear we don't ordinarily tote along.

A few days before a trip our living room is turned into a staging area. Anything that's going to be loaded into the RV is strategically placed in the living room according to where it will be packed in the RV.

Refrigerator food for the RV is loaded into the house refrigerator for pre-cooling.

As items are moved from the staging area and into the RV, they are checked off the list.

If we forget anything, we can buy it along the way or, as it usually turns out, we can do without.

56

Travel Library

"What travel reference books do you carry in your RV?"

Joe: Our most valuable reference book is our *Trailer Life Campground and RV Park Directory.*

We use this to locate RV parks and campgrounds along our travel route and those that are close to our destination. On travel days we look for a campground that is "easy in and easy out"; one that is conveniently located to the highway and has pull-through sites. When we are going to stay for any length of time, we pay attention to the width of the sites, amenities and scenic surroundings. Hookups (especially modem hookups), rates and the TL rating are also important to us.

The TL Directory also has helpful information about state laws and regulations regarding RVs on highways. The turnpike and tollway information can keep you legal. And the section on bridge, tunnel and ferry restrictions can tell you where you should not go. There is a section of Interstate 95, for example, that prohibits vehicles with propane containers.

Dump stations along major highways are identified in the TL Directory. This helpful section also lists those states that do not have dump stations in their rest areas as well as indicating those states that are preparing to remove their dump stations.

AAA campground directories are a good source of information on government campgrounds.

The *Kampground Of America* directory makes it convenient to locate these popular campgrounds. After locating a KOA in their directory, we check the TL Directory for their description and rating.

Vicki: The Rand McNally *Motor Carrier's Atlas* has become an important part of our route planning. We have a wide-body motorhome and RVs wider than 96 inches are not legal on all highways. The road maps in the *Motor Carrier's Atlas* highlights those roads where vehicles up to 102 inches are permitted.

We take AAA Tour Books for those states along our route of travel. They provide interesting information about the cities and towns we will visit. The tour books also list, describe and rate restaurants. We refer to the tour books when we are looking for a place to take our lunch break. Whenever possible, we like to stop at a location that offers a factory tour. They usually have an RV friendly parking lot and we get to combine lunch with an interesting tour.

A *Zip Code Directory* is a must for RV travelers. We use it to determine the zip code of the small town where we wish to receive mail. We try to choose a small town because the Post Office is easier to locate and parking our rig is seldom a problem. We know it is a small town if it has only one zip code. No matter what size town or how many zip codes it may have, we always call the Post Office at 1 (800) 275-8777 (ASK- USPS). The Post Office will confirm the zip code, tell us if we can receive mail at that branch and even tell us how to get there.

We also carry a *Flying J Travel Plaza Directory Map*. They have easy access RV fuel islands that provide both gasoline and diesel. RVs can be fueled from either side and the diesel pump's nozzle is not too large for the RV's fuel-filler opening. Flying J's sell propane and most have dump stations that may be used by RVers free of charge.

Emergency ID Card

Here is an RV travel and camping tip:

Create an emergency notification card to carry in your wallet. Have it identify two or more people who can be notified in case of an emergency. Be sure they are at different addresses and telephone numbers (one of them might not be available). Try to make sure these people know how to reach you when you are camping so they can notify you in an emergency. Furnish them an itinerary (even if its just a rough idea) if you can.

Your emergency notification card should also include the name of your traveling companion and the telephone number of his/her cellular phone. He/she might be sitting in your RV wondering why you have not returned.

Your emergency notification card should list any health problems, medications or allergies that paramedics and doctors should know about.

It is not a bad idea to have your telephone calling card number on your emergency notification card (but not identifying it as such). It might be convenient when you are under stress and want to place a call.

Some RVers carry a second emergency notification card that identifies their RV and the campground where they are staying. The card might even indicate if there are pets in the rig that need to be cared for.

How Much Cash?

"We are planning a coast-to-coast trip in our RV this summer. What about spending money on the road? How much cash should we carry? Should we take traveler's checks? What can we purchase with credit cards? We would appreciate any guidelines you can offer."

Joe: Only experience will tell you how much cash you need to have available. It depends upon your cash comfort level and spending habits. How important is it for you to pay with cash as opposed to using credit cards? How much cash do you want available to feel comfortable while you are on the road? Each person's needs and spending habits differ. There are a number of ways to deal with spending money on the road. We can tell you what we do. It works for us.

Vicki and I try to carry as little cash as possible in our motorhome and in our wallets.

Generally, we pay cash for purchases up to $10 or $15 and use our credit card for amounts higher than that.

We replenish our cash a couple of ways. One is by visiting an ATM and withdrawing enough cash to last us a week or two. Most RVers have found that ATMs are a convenient source of cash while traveling around the country. Check with the issuer of your ATM card to determine if your card can be used in the ATMs of other financial institutions. There is usually a fee associated with using these machines, so we try to minimize our visits by withdrawing a fairly large amount.

Our favorite way to get cash is to present our ATM/debit card when paying for groceries at a supermarket and ask for an additional $100 or so in cash. We have not been refused nor have we experienced any additional fee for this service.

Vicki: We use our credit card for the majority of our financial transactions. It minimizes our need for cash and provides a paper trail for our bookkeeping. At the end of the month we call the 800 number on the back of the card to determine the balance owed and minimum payment due. Obviously, paying the balance in full can eliminate any interest charges.

Most merchants accept credit cards. They can be used to pay for campgrounds, fuel, groceries, restaurant meals, and purchases of every description.

We do carry our personal checkbook when we travel. But, except to pay bills by mail, we rarely use it. Not too many merchants are willing to take an out-of-state personal check. We have discovered, though, that some campground operators actually prefer being paid by check rather than a credit card.

A modest amount of traveler's checks are stashed in our motorhome just in case we run into a situation where a personal check, credit card or our available cash will not cover a situation. I'm not sure how wise it is, though. The checks have been sitting there for five years now. That money could have been earning interest somewhere.

Cost of Fuel

"We are concerned that the skyrocketing cost of fuel will prevent us from enjoying our RV this summer. What's going on out there?"

Joe: We seem to go through this "price of fuel" crisis every so often. The fuel producers raise the price of fuel, the consumers squeal, the politicians make empty threats, the price of fuel comes down (but not very much), the consumer adjusts and life goes on.

Have you ever figured out how much you actually spend on fuel for your RV?

When our kids were in school and we were working 9:00 to 5:00 jobs, Vicki and I fell into the category of weekend/vacationers. We used our trailer an average of one weekend a month for seven months of the year. We also took an annual, two-week RVing vacation

Each of our weekends involved about 200 miles of round-trip travel. The two-week vacation was never more than 2,000 miles. That's a total of 3,400 RVing miles per year. About average for the RVer who is a weekend/vacationer.

Our Suburban got 10 miles to the gallon. Didn't matter whether it was towing or not. Going downhill, with the wind behind us and the engine turned off, it got 10 miles to the gallon. So our RV trips consumed about 340 gallons of gasoline a year.

Last year, we were quite content to pay $1.20 a gallon for fuel. Our RVing fuel would have cost about $408.00 if we were still weekend/vacationers.

As we write this column, gasoline is selling for about $1.70 per gallon. A little math tells us that this year our cost of RVing fuel would jump from $408.00 to about $578.00. That's an increase of $170.00. I don't think we would give up the pleasures of RVing for $170.00.

Vicki: Today, Joe and I are extended RV travelers. We go on the road for two to three months at a stretch. Since we are not pressed for time, our driving is not nesessarily destination oriented. Our travels, for the most part, allow us to enjoy the journey.

Over the years we have discovered that, for us, driving becomes tedious after six hours and downright miserable after eight. We rarely drive more than 300 to 400 miles a day. Most travel days we actually drive less than 250 miles. And, we don't drive every day.

Our diesel-powered motorhome averages 8 miles to the gallon. If we drive 300 miles, we consume about 38 gallons of fuel. If fuel costs $1.70 per gallon, it will cost us about $65.00 to travel that 300 miles.

The average cost for one night's stay in a commercial campground is about $20.00. Add that to the cost of a day's fuel and it would appear that we are paying $85.00 a day to travel in a motorhome.

But we don't travel every day. We may only travel for a day or two and then stay put in an interesting spot for two or three days. Some RV travelers remain in one location for a week or longer. When you are not traveling, you do not have any fuel expenses, only your daily campground fees.

To travel the 3,000 miles from San Diego to Boston we would consume 375 gallons of fuel at a cost of $638.00 (at $1.70 per gallon).

Even if we drove 300 miles a day, the trip would take us longer than ten days. Along the way we would spend time discovering and exploring the countryside.

Getting to Boston would take us at least three weeks. Spread out over 21 days, our fuel costs would average out to about $30.00 per day.

Add to that our campground fees of $20.00 a day and our RV trip is averaging about $50.00 a day for campgrounds and fuel.

Last year, when we paid $1.20 per gallon for fuel, our campground and fuel expenses would have been $42.00 a day. This year the same trip would cost an additional $8.00 a day. If the three-week journey was important to us we would find the $168.00.

Joe: There are a variety of ways to keep fuel costs to a minimum.

Reduce the number of miles you travel. Spend your weekends at campgrounds closer to home. Travel less and stay longer at vacation campgrounds.

Shop for fuel. Ask the campground operators and fellow RVers where the bargain fuel stations are located in the area. During your day trips away from the campground, check out the fuel stations and compare their prices. Use your CB radio to ask other RVers and truckers where the bargain fuel stops are located along your travel route.

When traveling cross country, plan your fuel stops so you purchase fuel in the states with the lower fuel taxes and thus, lower fuel prices (Arizona instead of California, for example).

Vicki: Of course, you always have the option of flying to your destination, renting a car and staying in a hotel. But then, that wouldn't be RVing.

Grocery Shopping Tips

"My husband and I plan to spend several months traveling in our motorhome. We're always looking for ways to save money. At home I know where the less expensive grocery stores are located and I can control the amount of money I spend on food. What can we do to reduce food costs on the road?"

Joe: When it comes to food shopping, my job is to push the shopping cart and carry in the groceries.

Vicki: Not only do we try to keep our food costs down, we are also aware of the differences in the foods that are available in various parts of the country. There are grocery items available at our home in Southern California that we know we won't be able to find in other places. We stock up on those items to take with us.

We always start out with several cans of Yuban coffee, for example. It's not available in other parts of the country. And, because we especially like Mexican food, we always begin with our freezer full of tortillas and chorizo. Enough to last throughout the trip.

As we travel, we try to make the most of the foods native to each section of the country. They usually cost less than in other areas. We look forward to the pork in Arkansas, citrus fruits in Florida, seafood along the coastal areas, peaches and pecans in Georgia and South Carolina. We love the roadside stands that sell fresh corn, tomatoes and other vegetables. Many work on the honor system, with just a sign telling the price of each item and a coffee can for purchasers to drop money into.

As you travel, you will also become familiar with the different chain supermarkets in the various parts of the country. I look for Shaw's in New England, Wegman's in the northeast, Kroger's in the mid-atlantic, Harris Teeter in the south, Publix in Florida, Meijer in the mid-west, Safeway in the west, Vons in Southern California, Fred Meyers in the northwest and, of course, Wal-Mart Supercenters all over the country.

We also have an assortment of supermarket-chain discount cards that provide additional savings. You name a supermarket with a discount card and I'll bet their card is in our RV.

I'm also a coupon clipper, whether at home or on the road. If I spot a store that doubles the value of coupons, I check it out. Every Sunday we buy a local newspaper. The grocery coupons more than pay for the newspaper. In addition, by glancing at the grocery ads for each store, we can get a feel for their prices. As a bonus, the newspaper provides us with a TV listing for the week. Not bad for $1.50!

Plan on spending more time grocery shopping on the road than you do at home. Brand names vary from one part of the country to another. It may take a while to figure out which to buy. Also, there doesn't seem to be a really consistent floor plan for supermarkets. We usually have to go up and down every single aisle to find what we're looking for.

Joe: And, once in a while, when Vicki isn't looking, I toss a bag of cookies into the grocery cart.

Locating Services

"Up until now we have only used our RV for weekend outings and two week vacations. On those brief trips we wait until we get home to do things like wash our rig, change the oil, get haircuts and go to a doctor. How do you find these services when you are on the road for extended periods of time?"

Joe: Most of the time, we ask the campground staff. A campground manager or ranger is usually a resident of the area and will tell you about the places they frequent. Campground hosts and staff, in many instances, are workampers (RVers who work temporarily at the campground). They understand your needs and will try to direct you to the location that will serve you best.

When you register, commercial RV parks and campgrounds usually provide you with a map of the campground. These maps often include a map of the community and advertisements placed by local businesses. Typically, the advertisements on campground maps will include RV service and repair shops, grocery stores, restaurants and drugstores. These merchants are telling you they are interested in doing business with RVers.

Vicki: There are a number of things you can do when it comes to getting medical attention. If you have a genuine emergency, go to the emergency room of a hospital. The campground staff can give you directions or, if necessary, call the paramedics. They will also guide the paramedics to your site.

If you do not have a real emergency, try to avoid going to an emergency room. You may have to wait while they take care of the real emergencies and your medical bill may be higher than if you went to a physician's office.

Once again, the campground staff may be able to direct you to a physician. Chances are they will tell you about their own doctor. That is a pretty good recommendation.

We have had very good experience with the Urgent Care, Walk-In Clinic type facilities that you find in shopping centers and strip malls. The clinics we have utilized have been great for minor ailments and injuries. We usually pay by credit card and wrestle with our insurance company when we get home.

Joe: Finding a facility to change the RV's oil and filters and to lubricate the chassis should not be all that difficult. We have talked to a number of RVers who have their rigs serviced at those quick-lube-while-you-wait type facilities. Many truck stops, like Flying J Travel Plazas, will also work on motorhomes.

Whenever possible, I prefer having our motorhome worked on by a facility that is acquainted with our type of vehicle, engine and drivetrain. RV dealerships that sell our particular model are an obvious location. Our motorhome is equipped with a Cummins engine and Allison transmission. I have found Cummins service centers in every area of the country. The work is accomplished in a facility that is equipped to handle large vehicles and has the type of lubricants and filters recommended for our rig.

Vicki: Our RV manufacturer provided us with a list of dealerships and service centers around the country. Working from the list we look to see where we will be in a week or so and then call to make an appointment.

Most service centers tell us to plan on leaving our motorhome for four to six hours. We take advantage of that time to do some shopping, visit a laundromat or go sightseeing.

Joe: Finding places to wash our motorhome is one of our biggest challenges. There are truck washing facilities along all the interstates. Most of them are happy to take our money and they do a good job. But I would much rather do the job myself. Not only is it good "therapy" for me but it gives me the opportunity to carefully examine every square inch of our motorhome.

Environmental and other considerations have just about eliminated the possibility of washing an RV in a campground. Every now and then, however, we run across a campground that will permit us to wash our rig. Sometimes we can wash it right at the site, other times there may be an RV washing area complete with a hose. We make a point of returning to those campgrounds whenever we travel.

Vicki: We also try to find a self-service car wash. One with sufficient overhead clearance so our motorhome will fit inside. The soap and water vending machine usually eats about $4.00 worth of quarters by the time we wash our motorhome and little car, but it is worth it.

Joe: Getting a haircut while traveling is pure trauma for me. At home, I go to a real man's barber. Striped barber pole out front. Sports Illustrated and antique National Geographic magazines in the waiting area. Men's hair products gathering dust on the shelf. After polite comments about the weather, the barber concentrates on the task at hand. Something I appreciate when a person is working on me with sharp instruments. Jim does an outstanding job. He is a skilled artisan. I'm out of there in less than 20 minutes.

One time, while traveling, Vicki talked me into going to a hair stylist that had done a good job on her hair. It was my first visit to a "Styling Salon". Redbook magazines, screaming hair dryers, clamoring voices, strange smells. Everyone was staring at me. Like them, I was wondering what a not-that-nice-a-guy was doing in a place like this.

When the receptionist (Jim doesn't have a receptionist) called out for "Mr. Kieva" the whole place went silent. Heads with funny things attached to them turned and followed me to the center chair. While Cindy washed my hair, the women on either side of me carried on a conversation that enlightened me as to the joys of childbirth, hysterectomies and varicose veins. Cindy's haircutting technique seemed to involve nothing more than random, yet rapid swipes with her scissors. She simultaneously treated me to a discourse on her dating and love life. I learned more about Cindy and her boyfriends than I really wanted to know. Forty minutes later I was breathing easier and sporting a decent haircut.

My next haircut on the road took place in a shop with a striped pole next to the door and a sign that boldy proclaimed "Barber". An old dog of questionable heritage shared a couch with equally vintage issues of Field And Stream magazines. Lots of masculine appeal. A real man's barber shop. Ten minutes in the chair, no conversation-- what more could I ask for?

Vicki: Joe was out of there in ten minutes all right... he looked like he had fallen in front of a lawn mower! Where was Cindy when he needed her?

Thank goodness, haircuts are not nearly as traumatic for me as they are for Joe. So much for female vanity! Fortunately, I only have to get a haircut every six weeks or so. In the meantime, I use my hair dryer and curling iron and do the best I can. When it's time for me to get a haircut on the road, I typically drive around and "stake out" a couple of styling salons. I have a firm rule--the sign out in front has to say, "Styling Salon". "Beauty Shop" or "Beauty Salon" just doesn't cut it. I sit in the car outside and watch the women as they come out. Then I go up to the window, peer in, and look at the "stylists". If they, or their clients have hair styles reminiscent of the 50's, I go elsewhere.

Unlike Joe, I can handle conversations about boyfriends, husbands, childbirth and hysterectomies. I can even add a few stories of my own!

Usually I walk away feeling pretty good about my haircut. Later, at home, I go to Shelley, the "stylist" that's been cutting my hair for 10 years. Invariably, she tells me what an awful job the last stylist did. I guess, for me, ignorance really is bliss!

Joe: When it comes to getting haircuts, it looks like you have your choice of asking the campground people for a recommendation or skulking around Styling Salons.

Where Are The Dump Stations?

"We did a considerable amount of house cleaning to our trailer after a recent trip. This resulted in filling our gray-water tank to the one-third-full mark. I drove to a local RV park and asked permission to use their disposal station. The owner said his disposal station was for paying customers. I offered to pay for the privilege and pointed out that we had camped there in the past. His rude reply was simply, "I'm not in the dump station business." Next stop was a franchise campground. A large sign on the disposal station proclaimed the disposal fee was $15.00 for non-campers. Further down the road was a state park with a campground. The ranger said he would have to charge me the day-use entry fee of $3.00 but that I could use the disposal station. Since then, other RVers have told me similar stories. What's going on?"

Joe: The campground business must be doing real well in your neck of the woods. You had two campground operators encourage you to take your future business to the state park.

What's going on is abuse. Abuse of disposal stations by a small percentage of RVers who are either ignorant or stupid (there's a difference). Unfortunately, as the number of RVers increases, so does the number of abusers.

Dump station abuse, in a nutshell, amounts to RVers making or leaving a mess or putting things into the dump drain that just do not belong there. Somebody has to clean up the mess or clean out the drain. That creates a health hazard, costs money and causes aggravation.

For years, RVers have been pulling into roadside rest areas or campgrounds and feeling free to use the disposal stations. Lately, thanks to the abusers, states have been eliminating dump stations from their rest areas, and campground operators now view their disposal stations as an expensive maintenance headache.

Ignorant RVers are just people who do not know any better. If you find yourself in the position of showing a new RVer how to use their rig, please include a few words about the proper way to use a disposal station or campground sewer hookup. Its just a few simple steps.

Drive up to the dump station. Open the sewer drain cover to be sure it's free of obstructions. Connect a sewer hose to the RV's sewer outlet and connect the other end to the sewer drain. If there is no connection at the sewer drain, put the other end of the hose about eight or nine inches into the sewer opening. Place your foot or a heavy object on the hose where it enters the drain to keep the hose from jumping out when the RV's drain valve is opened. The important point is to dump through a sewer hose and not onto the disposal station's apron!

Drain the black-water tank first. Later, the draining gray water will help clean the black water out of the sewer hose. When the black-water tank is empty, close the valve and pour two or three buckets of clean water into the toilet and drain the black-water tank again. Close the black-water tank valve and open the gray-water tank valve. While the gray water is draining, you can pour a bucket or two of clean water into the toilet and add some holding tank chemical.

When the gray-water tank is empty, close the valve. Now dissolve some holding tank chemical into a bucket of water and pour it into a sink or shower drain.

Rinse out your sewer hose with the non-potable water hose available at most dump stations. Do not rinse out your sewer hose with your drinking-water hose!

Now hose down the apron of the dump station.

Vicki: Here are a few tips to make dumping a little easier and faster. Try raising the curb side of the RV by driving up on leveling blocks or extending the leveling jacks. It might give you a faster and cleaner flush of your holding tanks.

Create a 6 to 8-foot length of sewer hose that can be conveniently used at dump stations. Carry a 10 to 12-foot length of old water hose to use when the dump station doesn't have one available (never connect it to a potable water faucet, and be sure to store it where it won't come into contact with your drinking water hose).

Whenever another RV is waiting to use the dump station, we forgo flushing the black-water tank and rinsing the sewer hose. We also pull forward and let the next RV move to the dump station before we add clean water and chemicals to the holding tanks. It's called common courtesy (now there is an oxymoron).

Never put anything into a sewer drain except the contents of your holding tanks, period. Leave the dump station cleaner than when you arrived. If there is a reasonable fee for using the disposal station, pay it and thank the operator for making the facility available. Remember, it costs money to install and maintain that dump station.

Joe: Stupid people are those who know better but still choose to be inconsiderate slobs. The stupid ones are the cause of diminishing free dump stations. And if they abuse free dump stations they probably abuse free overnight parking privileges too. Personally, we try to avoid associating with stupid people.

There are many disposal stations still out there. Most of them are free. Your *Trailer Life Campgrounds, RV Parks & Services Directory* has a list of free dump stations along interstates and highways. Most Flying J Travel Plazas have free dump stations adjacent to their RV fuel islands. Seek them out. Use them. But please, don't do anything stupid.

A propane water heater takes about half-an-hour and a considerable amount of propane to heat its six gallons of water. If you only need a small quantity of hot water in a short amount of time, use your electric coffee maker. Just make a pot of coffee without the coffee grounds. A 12 cup pot, should provide enough hot water to wash a small amount of dishes.

Lunch Stops

"When we only had brief vacations we got into the practice of being destination minded and traveling long distances. Now that we are retired we can't seem to break the habit. Our travel days are exhausting. How do other RVers get off the road?"

Joe: Our motto is "Enjoy The Journey" One of the things we do to make our daily travels entertaining is to find an interesting place to have lunch.

The only prerequisites are that it have a reasonably level place to park our rig, and offers free or nominal admission. We typically plan on spending a couple of hours.

Here are samples of the places we have taken our lunch breaks.

Community parks or playgrounds make great places to stop for lunch if you are traveling with children. It gives the kids something to look forward to during the morning, they can work off their pent up energy and they learn how to meet other kids. Sometimes the combination of lunch and exercise will result in a nap (theirs, not yours).

Factory outlet malls seem to be located along every interstate highway throughout the country. They give Vicki something to look forward to, release our pent-up cash and definitely result in me taking a nap.

Vicki: The smokejumper base off I-90 in Missoula, Montana, offers tours conducted by Forest Service firefighting smokejumpers. After listening to their first-hand accounts of parachuting into forest fires I found myself walking away muttering, "and they love it!"

Bonneville Lock and Dam on I-84 east of Portland, Oregon, has underwater windows that let you watch the salmon negotiating the fish ladders as they migrate upstream.

Natural Bridge north of Roanoke, Virginia, on I-81 offers a pleasant stroll along Cedar Creek to a natural arch. The spot where George Washington, father of our nation, carved his initials in the limestone wall can still be seen. I guess this also makes him the father of our graffitti "artists."

Wall Drug Store on I-90 in Wall, South Dakota, has become a famous stop for tourists. You'll see their entertaining roadside signs for miles in every direction. In addition to gobs of parking space (including a sign requesting aircraft to park at the airport), Wall Drug offers food, western gear and lots of gifts and souvenirs. It's still a drug store, too.

Presidential Libraries make good lunch stops. There usually seems to be plenty of parking. But some are so interesting we found ourselves spending the better part of an afternoon viewing the exhibits.

Check out small town museums, old U.S. Army cavalry forts and Spanish missions. they're usually pretty quiet and provide insight into the history of our country.

Our favorite lunch stops are the places that offer factory tours. We have tasted wines in California, toured lumber mills in the northwest, watched them make steel and assemble automobiles in the midwest, toured textile mills in New England, visited cigarette factories in the south and sampled beer in St. Louis.

Try stopping for lunch at places that look like they may be interesting. Stop at a few that don't look interesting (you may be surprised). In any case, get off the road, look around and...

Truckers

"During a class at a recent "Life On Wheels" Conference, you suggested we watch the truckers and benefit from their wisdom. Would you care to be more specific?"

Joe: RVers can learn a lot by carefully observing the truckers. Watch how they maneuver their big rigs. Pay attention to the way they position the backs of their trailers before backing into a loading dock or parking space. Notice, too, that they are not bashful about using a forward gear during the backing process.

Pay particular attention to how they make their turns. Observe how far from the curb they are when making a right turn and how far they pull into the intersection before actually beginning a turn.

Watch how truck drivers often move to the left of a vehicle parked on the right side of the road. The driver is considerately minimizing the impact of his air turbulance on the occupant of the parked vehicle. He is also creating a safety space for any unexpected activity that may suddenly occur around that parked vehicle; especially if it is an emergency vehicle or police car.

Notice how many trucks drive with their headlights on during the daytime. This is a safety practice that makes them more visible.

Also notice how truckers flash their lights when passing one another. The trucker being passed will flash his headlights on and off when there is room for the passing truck to return to the driving lane. The passing trucker will activate his right turn signal, move to the driving lane and then flash his running lights as a way of saying "thank you" to the trucker he just passed. This courteous behavior keeps a lot of trucks from bumping into one another.

Vicki: Before you decide to engage in this signaling practice, though, keep in mind there may be some liability on your part if you signal to a truck that it is safe to change lanes and it results in an accident. And don't forget how many trucks are driving with their headlights on during the daytime. You do not want to get into the habit of moving back to the driving lane just because you see the truck's headlights in your mirror. Learn to use your mirrors to accurately gauge when it is safe for you to make a lane change.

Speaking of mirrors, have you noticed the size, type, number and position of the mirrors on those big trucks? Professional drivers spend a lot of time paying attention to the traffic lanes on both sides of their rigs. They are also interested in where the rear of their trailer is in relationship to those lines painted on the road. A big truck's mirrors will extend out far enough to allow the driver to see the entire side of his trailer. There will also be at least one large convex mirror on each side that covers that "blind" spot just behind his cab doors. Truckers know, and RVers soon learn, that little "four-wheelers" seem to gravitate towards that blind spot.

Joe: Keep an eye on the traffic lanes selected by the majority of truckers. Chances are they have driven this road before and know which lane will get them to their destination with the least amount of hassle. And when you see a number of trucks in front of you suddenly changing from one lane to another, you do the same. In all likelihood they have just been alerted by CB radio of a road or traffic condition up ahead and they are moving into the best lane to get around it.

Listen to the trucker channel on your CB radio. It is channel 19 in most places; channel 17 on the west coast. Truckers spend a great deal of time trying to keep track of the police (also called bears, county mounties and other descriptive terms) along the highway.

Truckers will also use their CB radio to alert oncoming drivers to road hazards, traffic accidents and slowed or stopped traffic (they call it a brake check).

There have been a number of occasions when we have been able to select an alternate route, jump off the interstate and avoid a traffic jam by paying attention to these trucker advisories.

Vicki: Last known locations of police cars as well as locations of road hazards and traffic conditions are usually given in mile marker numbers. It's a good idea to become familiar with the mile markers along the side of the road.

If you are driving on an east/west interstate, the mile markers indicate how many miles you are from that state's western border. If you are traveling on a north/south interstate, the mile markers indicate the distance from that state's southern border. Pay attention to the little markers on the right side of the interstate highways. Their pattern will soon become clear to you.

Some (but not all) states number their interstate exits according to the nearest mile marker. Exit 12, for instance, will be located close to mile marker 12.

Knowing your exact location on an interstate can have some real advantages. If you call for assistance or to report an accident, the first thing you will be asked is your location. Being able to say "just north of mile marker 130 on the northbound side of Interstate 95" will speed the response of the appropriate agency.

Listening to the trucker's channel can be enlightening; you will learn a lot about truckers and the trucking business. It can be entertaining; truckers can tell some funny stories. It can also be scary. You will come to realize there are a few truckers and trucks (as well as RVers and RVs) that shouldn't be on the road. Hopefully, that awareness will keep you driving defensively.

As with all things, you have to take the good with the bad on the trucker's channel. Some truckers have something to say while others just talk a lot. There's a certain amount of garbage on the air but there are also 39 other CB channels for you to turn to.

Watch the truckers. There's a lot you can learn about driving and getting along on the road. Try to follow the example of the professional drivers. Avoid driving like the hotdoggers. And give the truckers a break. Make room for them to change lanes. Give them room to pass. Watch out for the truckers and you'll realize that, given the opportunity, they'll watch out for you.

Attach a spring-loaded clip on a suction cup to your windshield to hang your campground or rally pass.

Seatbelts

"We are planning a cross country trip and are wondering about the laws regarding seat belt use in motorhomes. Do they vary from state to state? We use seatbelts most of the time but wonder if it is legal for passengers to use the bathroom or get something from the fridge while under way. Is it legal or even wise for someone to sleep in the bedroom while the motorhome is moving?"

Joe: We didn't bother checking about the seatbelt laws in various states. We just assume that every state's vehicle code requires all occupants of a moving vehicle to be secured by a seatbelt. I am sure we will hear from readers if their state is an exception.

Years ago, when we went from a trailer to our first motorhome, it was not unusual for Vicki to move around while we were going down the road. She loved the idea of getting up, using the bathroom, grabbing a snack from the refrigerator and even taking a nap on the couch.

That motorhome had bunk beds. It was ideal for weekend camping trips with our kids. We would leave home on a Friday evening. The kids would climb into their bunks while we were enroute. They did not wake up until the next day. Sunday evening we planned our trip home so we would drive behind the heavy traffic. The kids would climb into their bunks for the journey home and, after we arrived, would spend the night in our driveway. That routine gave the kids (and us) two full days to enjoy the beach, mountains or desert.

Vicki: Then we started presenting seminars and teaching classes on RVing. We listened to our audience, students and the experts we consulted. We heard stories of quick stops that tossed unbelted passengers into furniture and through the windshield. We listened as a mother described the broken bones her children suffered when their motorhome rolled over. We read accident reports supplied by Highway Patrolmen that pointed out how the motorhome driver (belted in) walked away but the passengers were sent to the morgue.

We might have been ignorant but we are not stupid. Today we remain belted into our seats while the motorhome is under way. If we want to use the bathroom or get a snack, we stop at a roadside rest area or a wide spot in the road.

There is no need to see if the law requires you to use a seatbelt while your motorhome, camper, van or any other kind of vehicle is moving down the road. Common sense tells you to buckle up.

Camping With Non-RVers

"We want to travel in our trailer with another couple (they do not have an RV). Good friends that we are, we do not want to share the same sleeping quarters. Any suggestions?

Joe: We live in California; good friends of ours live in Arkansas. We are confirmed RVers; they are confirmed hotel folks. Each of us considers the other's method of travel as roughing it.

Once or twice a year we pick a place both couples want to explore and we meet there. We call ahead to campgrounds in the area to find out which hotels and motels are nearby. Our friends stay in the hotel and we stay in the campground. In many cases the hotel (or motel) and the campground are on the same grounds. We tour together during the day and retire to our respective living quarters at night. This system has worked for us in places like Las Vegas, New Orleans and Washington, DC. Our friendship seems to thrive on being able to share adventures without being in each other's hip pocket.

Vicki: Another way to travel in the same vehicle but have separate sleeping quarters, may be to look into the Kampin Kabins located in the KOA Kampgrounds. Some RV parks have rental trailers set up in some of their campsites.

You and your friends could share the transportation vehicle, your campsite and your trailer but still have the privacy of separate sleeping accommodations in the same campground.

RV Manners

"We are brand new to the world of RVing. Are there any rules of etiquette we should know about?"

Joe: Etiquette, or good manners, is simply being considerate of others.

I am one of those people who enjoys the sound of a campground in the morning. I love the rumbling of powerful engines coming to life, the crunch of tires rolling on gravel and the groans of trailer hitches taking up their loads. To me, it is the siren call of adventure. It makes me want to go.

However, I am not too fond of folks who leave loudly before 6 o'clock in the morning. Their preparations seem to always include lots of door slamming and tossing of leveling boards into truck beds. They run their engines interminably and suffocate the campground with exhaust fumes.

These must be the same people who arrive after 9 o'clock at night and can't seem to position themselves in their site without a lot of yelling and maneuvering. And, of course, their RVs are the ones with the loud exhausts and nerve-wracking back up beepers.

And then there is the guy who, after parking his RV as close as possible to my rig, extends both of his slideout rooms into my campsite. This person also seems to be the one whose leaking water or sewer hose creates a small lake under my picnic table.

I love watching the pet owners who take their dogs for a walk, pretend not to notice the animal pooping on the grass, and then immediately head back to their RVs. Who do they think they're fooling?

These same people are the ones who don't seem to notice that their dogs bark incessantly all day long. How do they stand living with an animal like that?

Vicki: I have no sympathy for people who abandon their clothes in campground washing machines or dryers and, when they return, find them piled in a corner. They should be there to retrieve their laundry when the load is finished.

Cellular phones have shortened if not eliminated the lines of people at pay phones. Still, I am grateful to the considerate people who limit the number of calls or the time spent on those calls when they see others waiting.

Now, the lines seem to be forming at the place where we plug in our laptops to pick up our e-mail. Veteran RVers have their computer programmed to dial the appropriate phone numbers before they plug into the data ports. They only stay online long enough to download (not read) their incoming e-mail and to send their prepared outgoing messages.

I do appreciate the professionalism of the RVer at the disposal station who attaches his sewer hose, pulls his valves (black then gray), disconnects his hose and immediately moves his RV out of the way so the next rig can pull into place.

You can bet he is also the person who moves his rig forward after he is finished fueling but before he goes inside to pay. This, by the way, is expected behavior at truck stops.

Joe: I am impressed by the master RVer who can pull into a campground late and leave early without making a sound; the thoughtful dog owners who not only clean up after their pets but care enough to teach them how to behave; the conscientious parents whose children make happy sounds at the playground and pool but don't run roughshod through my campsite. I am impressed by the majority of RVers and campers who have the good manners to be considerate of each other. It makes me want to stay.

Those large size containers of laundry soap and fabric softener may be economical to buy but they are difficult to store and a lot of weight to carry to the campground's laundry room. Buy the small or medium size containers

Meeting Other RVers

"We have just bought our first RV and are looking forward to camping in comfort. We enjoy meeting new people but don't wish to intrude on their privacy. How does one go about meeting other RVers?"

Joe: I think you will find you have to work at not meeting them. Most RVers and campers are pretty gregarious. To meet RVers, Vicki and I recommend that you take two walks around the campground every day. The first walk should take place after most of the travelers have arrived but well before nightfall. You will be able to look at the various types of rigs on the road and inspect the ingenious outside camping gear and gadgets that RVers can come up with.

This walk also provides an opportunity to meet new people. Just observe the body language of the campers who are outside. Some will be sitting way to the rear of their campsite with their backs to the road. These folks are not particularly interested in socializing at the moment. Other campers will be sitting under their awnings. They'll be facing the road, hats on the back of their head and have a drink in their hands. Their dogs will be wagging their tails. These folks are ready! A real giveaway is the guy who is sitting so close to the road he has to pull back his feet every time an RV passes by.

A sure fire conversation starter is "hello." Works every time. Follow that with an admiring word about their rig, dog or hat and you have just made a new friend. The most common questions in a campground are "Where are you from?" "Where are you going?" and "Where have you been?" Nobody cares what you do. It really isn't all that important.

The second walk of each day should be taken after dark. RVers have a tendency to leave their blinds open for an hour or so after dinner. Now you have the opportunity to see how they have decorated the interior of their rigs and to see if they have the good sense to drink your brand of bourbon. Both of these subjects make excellent conversation starters when you see them outside the next day.

Vicki: Many campgrounds and RV parks create opportunities for their guests to socialize. They conduct campfires with singing, story telling and other forms of entertainment. We've also seen quilting bees, exercise classes and craft fairs offered at RV parks and campgrounds.

The campground laundry room is one of my favorite places to meet RVers. If you are waiting for your clothes to wash or dry, you might as well start talking to the others who are waiting for their clothes.

This is an excellent way to find out what's down the road. We have gotten some of our best camping and traveling information from people we've met in campground laundry rooms. There is a fifty-fifty chance that the people you are talking with have just come from the direction you are heading. They can tell you about road and traffic conditions, campgrounds, tourist attractions and good places to eat.

Speaking of places to eat. You will discover that a number of campgrounds offer morning coffee, doughnuts, breakfasts, barbecues and dinners right on their grounds. We have observed that many KOA campgrounds are offering their guests the opportunity to buy their morning or evening meal without the bother of leaving the campground. What better place to socialize with fellow campers than over a meal?

Start with "hello." You will discover that RVers are the nicest bunch of people in the world.

Losing a purse or wallet can be twice as devastating when you are traveling. Next time you are near a copy machine, make a couple of copies of your driver's license, credit cards, insurance cards and other important papers in your wallet.

Make a note of the telephone numbers you should call if your credit cards, etc. are lost or stolen. Store one set of the copies in your safe at home and another in a safe spot in your RV.

If you do lose your wallet or purse you will now have the information you need to cancel the lost credit cards and arrange for duplicates of your other documents.

Plug-in electric timers can be used to start your coffee in the morning or to turn an interior light on and off when you are absent.

RV Security

"We are planning a six month RV tour of the North American continent. We will have to fly home on a couple of occasions to attend the weddings of close relatives. Any suggestions of what we can do with our fifth-wheel while we are gone?"

Joe: Even though we consider flying and staying in hotels as roughing it, several times a year we end up parking our motorhome in a campground while we fly to an RV show to present seminars. Here is what has worked for us.

Try to select an RV park in a decent area that is well maintained. If it advertises "security," all the better. Talk to the owner or manager. Explain that you will be gone and are concerned about the security of your RV. In many cases the manager has parked our rig in the site next to his own RV or next to the office where they could keep an eye on it.

Vicki: Although it costs a few dollar more, get an electrical hookup. That way you can leave your refrigerator running.

For additional security you might try leaving a radio (at a low volume) and table lamp on a timer.

Finally, prevent any chance of water damage by shutting off the water at the campground faucet and turning off your RVs water pump.

There are no guarantees in life but chances are you will return to find your RV just as you left it.

Weather-Wise RVing

North America experiences some of the most severe weather in the world. Hurricanes, tornadoes, thunderstorms, lightning, hail and torrential rains are natural occurrences.

You can cancel a weekend camping trip if the weatherman predicts bad weather. But, if you are already on vacation, or if you are traveling far from home, you have no choice but to deal with whatever Mother Nature decides to throw at you.

Fortunately, most severe weather episodes last only a brief amount of time. And, to most RVers, they are only a slight inconvenience. But, severe weather can result in serious injury and even death.

Weather-wise RVers are able to take the precautions that maximize their safety during severe weather.

Rain can limit visibility (both yours and other drivers') and create slick driving surfaces. Water on the road can also conceal hazards such as deep potholes.

Turn on both your windshield wipers and headlights. Slow down. Increase the distance between your rig and the vehicle in front of you. Don't be afraid to get off the highway until conditions improve.

Keep in mind that heavy sustained rain can cause flash floods. Avoid parking in dry stream beds, ravines or low-lying areas when heavy rain is predicted.

It is a good idea to start each travel day with a clean windshield and windshield wipers.

Wind is the one weather condition that can't be seen. When the weather reports start mentioning winds of 15 to 20 mph, consider it a warning. Sidewinds of 15 mph and their accompanying gusts can adversely affect the handling of our high-profile vehicles. And it is not just the RV you are driving that the wind is pushing from lane to lane. Do you really want to risk having the other guy blown into you?

By the way, winds are named for the direction they are coming from. A north wind, for example, is blowing from the north.

Watch the treetops, grass, flags, dust and other indicators to determine the wind direction and velocity.

Observe the movement of high-profile trucks, trailers and motorhomes driving in front of you. A sudden sideways movement by one of them could indicate a gusting wind area ahead.

Be prepared for gusts of side winds when you pass trucks, cross bridges, exit tunnels or move from the protection of a hill to an open area of highway.

Pay close attention to "wind advisories" on the radio. If it is too windy for an 18-wheeler, it is certainly too windy for an RV.

Heavier vehicles and those with longer wheelbases will fare better in sidewinds than others. Ultimately, it is your responsibility to determine at what point you should get off the highway.

You can present a minimum profile to the wind by parking your rig so it faces into or away from the wind. Keep in mind, though, that parking so your RV faces into the wind could expose its windshield to damage from flying sand and debris.

Whenever possible, seek shelter from the wind and blowing debris in the downwind side of a large object such as a building or big-rig truck. Recognize, however, that strong winds can blow shingles and debris from the roof of the building. And that big truck may decide to leave before it is safe for you to do so.

Thunderstorms occur in every part of the nation; more in some areas than in others.

Increasing wind, flashes of lightning and thunder are what distinguish a thunderstorm from a hard rain.

Diminished visibility, slick roads and strong winds make driving in a thunderstorm an extremely hazardous undertaking. Get off the road.

Be careful where you park. The combination of rain-soaked ground and high winds can topple tall trees and heavy rainfall can lead to flash flooding.

Lightning is produced by every thunderstorm. A lightning bolt causes the surrounding air to rapidly heat and expand. That rapid expansion of air creates the shock wave we hear as thunder.

When lightning is close by, it sounds like a sharp crack. Lightning at a distance produces growling, rumbling sounds.

You can measure the distance between yourself and a lightning bolt by counting the seconds between the time you see the lightning and the time you hear its thunder. Every second is equal to about one-thousand feet. If you count five seconds between a flash of lightning and the sound of its thunder, the lightning is 5,000 feet, or about one mile, away.

No matter the distance, if you can hear thunder, you are probably close enough to the storm to be struck by lightning.

Lightning takes the shortest path between the cloud and the earth. It hits the tallest object available. So, it only makes sense that you should avoid being higher than the surrounding landscape. Do not stand (or park) under a natural lightning rod such as a tall tree or power pole in an open area.

Lightning can strike telephone lines and shock people on nearby phones. Restrict your usage of wired telephones to emergencies.

Lightning can strike power lines and damage electronic equipment. Avoid using electric appliances during a thunderstorm. RVers can avoid damage to their rig's equipment and appliances by disconnecting from the campground's electric, cable and telephone hookups.

Lightning can strike metal fences and plumbing. Stay away from them

Lightning can strike water, shocking everything in it. Get out of and away from open water.

If you are outside, do not carry metal objects. Put down that golf club. Take cover inside a house, large building or an all-metal vehicle.

If you feel your hair stand on end (which indicates lightning is about to strike), squat down or drop to your knees, bend forward and put your hands on your knees. **Do not lie flat on the ground** because wet ground can carry electricity.

Hail is another byproduct of thunderstorms. Large hail can damage windshields, dent the roofs of cars, penetrate plastic roof vent covers, collapse awnings and inflict bodily injury. Do not go outside during a hailstorm.

If you are driving, get safely off the highway and stop. Stay inside your vehicle. Hailstorms typically do not last very long.

Large hail could mean that a tornado is nearby. Turn on a radio or television and pay attention to weather advisories.

Tornadoes are violently rotating columns of air which descend from a thunderstorm cloud system.

Tornadoes are rare in many parts of the country but they have occurred in all 50 states.

Atmospheric conditions that produce tornadoes are most favorable in the deep south and the broad, flat basin between the Rocky Mountains and the Appalachians

Tornadoes can occur at any time of the year. Statistically, though, most tornadoes take place in April, May and June with May being the peak month. The least number of tornadoes occur in January and February

The gulf states experience most of their tornadoes from January through April with a second peak in October and November.

The central states (which include tornado alley) seem to have most of their tornadoes from March through June.

Tornado Alley is said to be the place where tornadoes hit most in the United States. It is that area of the country that encompasses northeast Texas, the eastern sections of Oklahoma and Kansas and the western portions of Missouri and Iowa. (Interstate 35 from Dallas, Texas to Des Moines, Iowa seems to follow tornado alley.)

Statistically, most tornadoes strike between 4:00 pm and 9:00 pm but they can strike any time of the day or night.

Most tornado injuries and deaths are caused by flying debris.

If you spot the funnel cloud of a tornado while in your vehicle, and if the tornado is at a distance, drive away from its path at a right angle. If it is close, get out of your vehicle. An RV offers little, if any, protection from a tornado. Take shelter in a building or lie flat in a ditch or culvert. Your objective should be to protect yourself from the flying debris (which could include your RV).

Do not seek shelter under a highway overpass. A National Weather Service meteorologist explained that tornado winds, squeezing under an overpass, increase by as much as 25%. Flying debris will strike with more force and you can be blown away.

If you are in a building, take cover on the lowest floor (preferably the basement) in the middle of the house. Go to a narrow interior hallway, a windowless room or closet. Face the wall. Crouch down and cover your head with your arms. Again, the idea is to protect yourself from breaking windows and flying objects.

Gymnasiums, auditoriums and other buildings with wide, free-span roofs are not the best shelters against tornadoes. There is a danger the roof might collapse

Hurricanes approach the eastern US from the southeast Atlantic. The ones that reach the east and gulf coasts typically turn north and east when they strike land.

The six-month Atlantic hurricane season officially begins June 1 and ends November 30. The majority of hurricanes have historically formed during August, September and October with September being the peak time.

Hurricanes generally lose their strength after making landfall but they frequently send powerful thunderstorms inland.

RVers have the advantage of being able to move hundreds of miles inland when the weather service predicts a hurricane.

If you can't escape the hurricane, move inland or away from the shoreline to avoid the storm surge (a wall of water pushed ashore by the storm).

Flying debris and falling objects are two of the major hazards of a hurricane. Take cover.

Precautions should be an everyday occurrance for RV travelers.

Pay attention to the long-range weather forecasts. If a hurricane is predicted to strike southern Florida, that is not the time to visit the Florida Keys.

Be aware of local weather conditions by listening to the local weather forecasts broadcast on television and radio.

Keep in mind, while watching weather reports, that most storms and tornadoes move from the southwest to the northeast

Weather alerts broadcast by radio and television stations usually provide the names of the counties that may be affected. Most RV travelers, though, have no idea of the name of the county in which they are located.

When registering at a campground, ask what county the campground is in. This is also a good time to ask which TV station is best to watch during severe weather and where the campground's storm shelter (if any) is located. Write the information on the campground's site map. Keep it handy.

Buy and learn how to use a weather radio that will receive National Weather Radio transmissions.

National Weather Radio (NWR) is provided as a public service by the National Oceanic and Atmospheric Administration (NOAA). Its nationwide network of radio stations broadcasts regional weather information 24 hours a day. The messages are repeated every five minutes or so and updated at least every two or three hours.

National Weather Radio usually requires a special radio to pick up its broadcasts. These radios, available at electronic stores such as RadioShack, are either battery operated or AC powered with a battery backup. Other radios might also be equipped to receive NWR broadcasts. Obviously, a battery-powered radio is a must during severe weather conditions.

An NWR radio can be as easy to use as turning it on and moving a tuning switch among three channels to find the one with the strongest signal. NWR broadcasts on seven frequencies so a better choice might be a radio that can tune into all seven. Most NWR radios are equipped with an alert feature that sets off an alarm when a severe weather alert is issued.

Understand the difference between a weather "watch" and a weather "warning"

A tornado **watch**, for example, means conditions are favorable for the development of tornadoes. A tornado **warning** means a tornado has been spotted or is imminent.

When a "watch" is issued, Be alert - take precautions, Ask where the nearest shelter is located. When a "warning" is broadcast for your location, take cover!

Weather-wise RVers remain alert to changing weather conditions; do what they can to avoid severe weather situations; and take appropriate action to safely ride out anything that nature decides to throw at them.

We pay attention to television weather reports; look at a USA Today weather page every couple of days or so and ask the campground operators what the weather looks like.

When the weather looks threatening, we periodically turn on our weather radio for the NWS regional weather report.

Don't get paranoid about severe weather. We have been RVing for over 35 years. We make two round-trip, cross-country trips each year. In all that time we have seen three tornadoes (all on the same day), changed plans to avoid a hurricane once, sat through no telling how many thunder and lightning storms and sweated out a few tornado watches. We have never experienced what we would term a close call. In fact, just about all of our disagreeable weather has been in the form of overcast skies, rain or temperature extremes (above 85 degrees or below 65 degrees).

Be weather-wise and enjoy the journey.

The Weather Channel has a web site: www.weather.com

Sanitary Hookups

"Is there a correct procedure for connecting an RV to utility hookups and for dumping holding tanks? Should any hygienic precautions be followed?"

Joe: You've hit one of my hot buttons. I am concerned about sanitary conditions, especially around the water hookup. Let me tell you why.

It's not unusual to see birds, squirrels and dogs lick the moisture from a campground faucet. We have also seen birds use faucet handles as outhouse perches with the predictable outcome.

But it's the human squirrels that bother me. One time an RV pulled into a site next to ours. Two dogs bounded outside and, with canine enthusiasm, began investigating their surroundings.

Once they had checked out the coolers, picnic tables and fire rings of their neighbors, the dogs proceeded to "tag" the boundaries of their territory. It turned out that one cornerstone of their new homestead was a post supporting a water hookup faucet. First one dog, then the other, lifted a leg to salute and annoint the post and, coincidentally, the faucet.

The RVer, oblivious to the antics of his untethered pets, eventually attached his RV's water hose to that faucet. Justice has a sense of humor.

Vicki: A lot of people don't seem to realize that harmful bacteria can be picked up on their hands from a sewer hose and transferred to a drinking-water hose. We see too many RVers hook up or disconnect their water hoses with bare hands that have just been soiled from handling their sewer hoses.

Or they don gloves to protect their hands while handling the sewer hoses but fail to remove them while handling their drinking-water hose. And, of course, those moist, bacteria laden gloves are then stored in a warm, dark compartment where the bacteria can multiply.

Joe: I watched a man dump his holding tanks, place the dripping sewer hose in his rig's side compartment and then toss a very expensive water purifier on top of the sewer hose. Excuse me! Is anyone home?

Then there's the guy who rinses out his sewer hose with his drinking-water hose. I have seen as much as two feet of drinking-water hose get inserted into a sewer hose. That's dumb!

Worst of all, we have seen a number of RVers use the campsite water faucet to rinse out their sewer hose. And, of course, to do the job properly the faucet had to be put inside the sewer hose opening. That's dumb and inconsiderate.

Vicki: Everyone seems to have their own routine for hooking up their utilities. Ours is designed to protect ourselves from what Joe calls (among other things) the oblivious, the dumb and the inconsiderate.

Before leveling our rig we check the electric outlet's polarity, the water's clarity and the sewer inlet's availability (mischievious beer cans and rocks occasionally crawl into and block the opening). Next, we rinse off the campground's faucet and spray it with a household disinfectant. By the time we finish backing and leveling the rig, the disinfectant, hopefully, has had time to accomplish its purpose.

Joe: I prefer to connect the electric hookup first, while the ground and my hands are dry. Turning off the electric outlet's breaker switch before inserting or removing the RV's electric plug can prevent shocks to the RVer and avoid damage to the prongs of the plug.

Next I connect the water-pressure regulator to the campground faucet so it can protect the water hose as well as the RV's plumbing. The water filter (optional) is next, followed by the water hose. I run water through the hose to remove the air, then attach the hose to the RV.

The sewer hookup is last. When handling the sewer hose I prefer to wear disposable polyethylene gloves that can be thrown away after use. They come in boxes of 100, are inexpensive and can be used for a variety of dirty jobs. Some RVers use disposable, latex surgical gloves. Even with the gloves, I wash my hands with antibacterial soap immediately after handling the sewer hose.

The gray-water tank's valve is opened after the sewer hose is connected. The black-water tank's valve remains closed until I am ready to dump. A day or so before dumping the black water, I close the gray water valve. The captured gray water will be used to rinse the sewer hose after I dump the black-water tank.

Dumping the holding tanks is pretty straight forward. We have found that raising the curb side of our RV produces a better flush. Black water is dumped first, the valve closed and then the gray water is dumped. The gray water does an excellent job of rinsing the black water out of the sewer hose. Raising the hose at the RV end drains the remaining water into the campground's sewer.

After closing the black water valve and capping the RV's sewer outlet, the hose is stored in the sewer hose compartment. A two-gallon bucket is used to pour a few gallons of water through the toilet bowl and into the black water tank. This prevents any solids from turning into a low-grade cement in the bottom of the tank.

Occasionally, after dumping and before driving to the next campground we put six to eight gallons of water and some liquid soap into both holding tanks. Both tanks are dumped when we arrive at the next campground. We have just washed out our holding tanks.

We disconnect in the same order we hooked up; electric first, water next and sewer last.

We connect both ends of the drinking-water hose together to keep moisture in and critters out. The water hose and fixtures are stored in a separate compartment from the sewer hose and its attachments.

Vicki: While Joe is dumping and disconnecting in preparation for us to leave a campsite, I secure the interior of the RV. One of the things I do is put the RV's trash bag in the doorway so he can take it to the dumpster. He simply adds the disposable gloves to the bag.

There is no one "correct" procedure for connecting to a campground's utility hookups. I'm sure some will look upon ours as being close to paranoia while others will say we are not cautious enough. The important thing is to develop a routine and an awareness that prevents contamination, avoids electrical shocks and keeps your feet dry.

Electric Hookup Basics

Hooking up to a campground's electrical connection is pretty straight forward. You simply plug the RV's electric cord into the campground's electric outlet. Just like plugging a toaster into your kitchen's electric outlet.

Joe: The campground's electric outlet (hookup) is usually located inside a gray metal box mounted on a post or pipe adjacent to your campsite. Inside the box you will find different size electrical outlets. There are variations but, typically, there will be a 20-amp outlet, a 30-amp outlet and a 50-amp outlet. Don't be surprised, though, if you find only one or two outlets.

The 20-amp outlet resembles the electrical outlets in your home. It will accept the plug of a common household extension cord. 20-amp electrical service is usually adequate to operate one major household appliance such as a convection oven, toaster or hair dryer.

The 30-amp outlet is a little larger than the 20-amp. It is designed for the plug found at the end of an RV's 30-amp hookup cord. This is the most common electrical outlet in today's RV parks and campgrounds. 30-amp electrical service is usually sufficient to operate two major appliances at the same time.

The 50-amp outlet is a bit bigger than the-30 amp. It will accept the plug of an RV's 50-amp cord. Many of today's larger motorhomes and trailers require 50-amp service to comfortably operate all their electrical appliances and equipment. 50-amp outlets can usually be found in newer RV parks and campgrounds as well as those that have had their electrical service upgraded.

Don't let all these outlets confuse you. The plug on your RV's electric cord will only fit into the appropriate outlet.

A breaker switch is usually located above or to the side of each of these electrical outlets. The breaker switch resembles the light switch you would find on the wall of your home. Just like your home's light switch, when the breaker switch is in the down position the electrical power to the outlet should be off. When the switch is in the up position, the power to the outlet should be on.

The words "on" and "off" are inscribed on each breaker switch to reveal its position. Be sure you read the inscription when determining whether the power is on or off.

Vicki: The majority of today's RVs are equipped for 30-amp service. The RV end of the 30-amp cord is usually permanently connected inside the RV cabinet where the cord is stored.

On most RVs equipped for 50-amp service, however, one end of the 50-amp cord has to be connected to a receptacle on the outside wall of the RV, the other end is then plugged into the campground outlet. 50-amp cords are considerably bulkier, heavier and more difficult to handle than 30-amp cords.

The proper electrical hookup procedure for both 30-amp and 50-amp RVs is to move the campground's breaker switch to the "off" position, uncoil the electrical cord, plug into the appropriate outlet and then return the breaker switch to the "on" position.

There may be instances when your electric cord's plug will not fit the available outlet. There are adapters available for these occasions.

Those whose RVs have a 30-amp cord will want an adapter that permits them to connect to a 20-amp outlet. On rare occasions they may appreciate an adapter that allows than to connect to a 50-amp outlet.

Those with 50-amp cords will definitely need an adapter that allows them to connect to 30-amp service. An additional adapter that connects the 30-amp adapter to a 20-amp outlet may also come in handy.

In over 35 years of RVing, we have had only two instances when we needed an adapter that would permit us to plug a 20-amp extension cord into a 30-amp outlet.

Every RV owner will appreciate having a 25-foot, 30-amp extension cord for those occasions when the campground's electrical hookup is beyond the reach of their RV's regular electric cord. 50-amp extension cords are also available, but their cost and the storage space they occupy may not be justified by the number of times you will use them. It is easier to simply connect the 50-amp cord to the 30-amp extension cord using an adapter.

While it is unusual to run across an improperly wired electrical outlet in a campground, it does happen. Before connecting the RV's electric cord, check the campground's electrical outlet with a circuit analyzer (also called a polarity checker). You simply plug it into the outlet. The analyzer should warn you of any irregularities. Ask for another campsite if the circuit analyzer indicates the outlet is defective.

Joe: Another handy device is a voltage meter. Plug it into an electrical outlet inside your RV and it tells you how much voltage is available. We leave our voltage meter plugged into an outlet where it is easy to monitor. Whenever it reads lower than 105 volts we turn off our motorized appliances. Motorized appliances, such as the air-conditioner and the washer/dryer can be damaged if they are operated on less than 105 volts. Operating high wattage equipment on low voltage could also create a fire hazard.

Locate your RV's electrical (breaker) panel. With any luck the manufacturer has identified the electrical circuits (outlets, air conditioners, microwave, etc) served by each circuit breaker. Each circuit-breaker switch will be inscribed with the amperage load it will carry.

If your RV has a 30-amp electrical system and is plugged into a campground's 30-amp outlet, you should be able to draw up to 30 amps of electricity. If you draw more than 30 amps of power it is possible for the wiring in your RV, your hookup cord or the campground's electric hookup box to heat up to the point of starting a fire.

When the amperage demands exceed the circuit-breaker's limit, the circuit-breaker should "trip" (open), and discontinue electric service to that circuit. In most cases the circuit-breaker is tripped because the RVer is operating too many appliances on that circuit. One 30-amp circuit, for example, may be overloaded if you try to operate a toaster, electric heater and hair dryer at the same time.

Vicki: If you experience a sudden unexplained power loss, turn off the appliances and go to the RV's electric panel. Look closely to see if one of the switches is not completely in the "on" position. Move the switch completely to "off" and then back to "on." You have found the problem if the power comes back on. Now try operating one or two less appliances on that circuit.

If the RV's circuit breaker continues to trip, there could be a "short" or other damage in the circuit. Seek the assistance of an RV service technician.

If there is a power loss and the circuit breakers in the RV's electrical panel are all on, check the circuit breakers in the campground's hookup box. A tripped circuit breaker here means your RV is drawing more electricity than the campground's hookup is designed to deliver.

If the problem is not at the circuit breakers, chances are the problem lies elsewhere and your RV neighbors are also without power. Notify the campground management.

Before you do, though, don't overlook the obvious. The problem may be that the appliance or the RV hookup has simply come unplugged.

Joe: To prevent the circuit breakers from opening, keep your amperage draw within the amperage rating of your RV's electrical system or the campground's hookup, whichever is lower.

You can do this by determining the amperage draw of each of your appliances. Look on the back or bottom of the appliance (or in its instruction book) and locate its wattage rating. A hair dryer, for example, may say 1500 watts (or 1500w). Divide the number of watts by 120 volts to determine how many amps the appliance draws. In this case, the hair dryer draws 12.5 amps while operating.

It is a good idea to maintain a list of all the appliances in your RV that draw 120-volt electricity and the amount of amperage each one draws. The list should include the air-conditioner, microwave/convection oven, washer/dryer, electric water heater, plug-in space heater, toaster, coffee maker, iron, hair dryer, refrigerator, etc.

Now, by applying a little math, you can be sure the total number of amps you draw does not exceed the amperage number on the circuit breakers on your RV's electrical panel or the circuit breakers in the campground's hookup box.

Remember, the amount of amps you draw should not exceed the amperage of the campground's electrical outlet

108

or the RV's electrical hookup cord, whichever is <u>lower</u>. In other words a 50-amp cord connected to a 30-amp outlet should not attempt to draw more than 30 amps. Nor should a 30-amp cord connected to a 50-amp outlet attempt to draw more than 30 amps.

Public pay phones are still a popular way of keeping in touch with home while you are on the road. Before you make your call, however, be sure you access your own long distance carrier. There are some independent phone companies whose payphones charge outrageous amounts for long distance calls.

Propane: On or Off?

"We keep getting conflicting opinions about operating our RV's refrigerator on propane while driving down the highway. What do you do?"

Joe: For 25 years we drove all over the country with our RV refrigerator operating on propane. The refrigerator worked fine and we never had any problems.

One day, a participant in one of our seminars described an RV fire that occurred when her trailer was struck by an out of control automobile. Initially, the damage was minor. Then the propane, escaping from a ruptured pipe, was ignited by the refrigerator flame. The rest of the story wasn't pretty.

Later, another seminar participant, a fireman, told of witnessing two gas station fires that were started when the fumes from spilled gasoline reached the flame of RV refrigerators operating on propane.

We heard those stories eight years ago. Since then we have made a habit of turning off our propane at the tank before driving down the road. We still haven't experienced any problems.

You will encounter bridges and tunnels around the country that won't allow you to cross or enter them until your RV's propane is turned off at the tank. Some bridges and tunnels prohibit any vehicles that even have propane tanks. All the ferries we have been on tell you to turn off the propane. Then they check to see if it is done and put a seal on the tank valve to show compliance.

The way we look at it, something disastrous must have occurred in the past to encourage those restrictions.

Vicki: Usually, before going on the road, we just turn the refrigerator to "off", turn off the propane at the tank and that's it.

By the way, before turning off the propane at the tank, be sure to turn off all the propane-operated appliances at the appliance. They may be equipped with electronic re-igniters. If the appliance is not turned off, these igniters will repeatedly emit a spark when the appliance's flame goes out. They don't know the propane is turned off; they only know the flame is out and their job is to re-ignite the propane. That spark, just like the refrigerator flame, could ignite any stray gasoline or propane fumes.

The food in our refrigerator has always remained cold for the six to eight hours the refrigerator is off. Just in case, here are a few tips that will help keep your refrigerator cool even though it is not operating:

Prevent the loss of cold air from the refrigerator by not opening its door more often than necessary. When you do open the door, close it as soon as possible.

The evening before a travel day, turn the refrigerator thermostat down so you can super-cool (but not freeze) the refrigerator's contents.

Keep two or three containers of refreezable "blue ice" in your RV's freezer. Move one or two of them to the top shelf of the refrigerator compartment when you turn the refrigerator off. Return the "blue ice" to the freezer compartment when you turn the refrigerator back on.

When driving on hot days, we frequently turn on our generator to run our motorhome's roof air conditioners. We operate our refrigerator on AC electricity at the same time.

Turning off the appliances and propane before heading down the road may seem a bit of a bother. And, at first, you will probably hold your breath wondering if the refrigerator contents will remain cold. Soon, just like lowering the TV antenna, it will become a part of your travel routine. And you will relax when you discover that your food stays cold.

Joe: Dealing with reality, we know that the majority of RVers leave their refrigerator running on propane while they travel. If you are one of them, please... before you pull into a gas station, turn off your refrigerator's flame. We might be sitting in the fuel island next to you.

Refrigerator: On Or Off?

"When the refrigerator is not in use should it be left on or off?

Joe: The answer is "it depends."

Vicki: When we put our RV into storage between trips we turn the refrigerator off, remove all the food, clean the interior and leave the door slightly ajar. We also disconnect the coach batteries and turn off the propane at the tank.

When we prepare the RV for the next trip we turn on the refrigerator, close its door and let it cool down before loading it with food that we have pre-cooled in our house refrigerator.

There are times when we leave our RV unoccupied in an RV park for as long as 10 days. If there is food in the refrigerator that won't spoil while we are gone, we leave the refrigerator operating on electricity. If the refrigerator is empty, we turn it off and leave the door ajar.

During these brief absences we also turn off the propane at the tank and turn off the water at the campground faucet.

Joe: Like I said, it all depends.

Water Filters

"What, if anything, do you do about water filtration in your RV? I have seen everything from no filters to elaborate purification systems."

Joe: We went for many years without filtering the water we put into our RV. Once in a while I would attach an inexpensive, sediment filter to our water hose but it seemed like such a bother. After all, I reasoned, the campgrounds were either on treated city systems or their well water was tested periodically. And if the owner/operators of the campground consumed that water it must be safe for me.

Besides, I always look at, smell and taste the campground's water before I hook up to it. In over 35 years we've run across only three campgrounds whose water failed my look, smell and taste test.

Vicki: But Joe's eyesight and sense of smell isn't what it use to be. And no one has ever accused him of having good taste (except for marrying me, of course). So when we took delivery of our new RV we decided to filter all the water that went into it.

We looked at an overwhelming variety of water filtration and treatment systems. Judging by the sales literature it was a miracle we had survived all the "bad" water we had been ingesting these many years.

Traveling as we do, our water comes from a variety of sources with the potential of being contaminated.

Reason seemed to suggest that some kind of filtration system was in order but experience indicated we could get by without spending a small fortune.

We considered the substances (dead and alive) we wanted to eliminate from our drinking water and researched the filters that would accomplish the job.

Joe: We installed a sediment filter on our exterior water hose. Its purpose is to screen out any dirt, rust or other particles from all the water going into our rig.

The sediment filter does not affect the chlorine content of the water that reaches our RV's water tank or plumbing. Chlorine kills bacteria. We wanted that protection to continue in our water system, especially in our water tank.

A second filter was installed on the cold water line to our kitchen faucet. It meets NSF Standard 43, is Certified Class I and uses solid block carbon. This one is designed to reduce or eliminate bad taste and odors (like chlorine), chemicals, cysts, lead and heavy metals. It is also bacteriostatic, which means it is constructed of materials that prevent the growth of bacteria within the filter itself.

This filter setup screens sediment from the water as it enters our rig, allows the chlorine to continue battling with bacteria and gives us reasonably acceptable water for drinking and food preparation.

We change the inexpensive, outside sediment filter every three months and the under sink filter about every six months (we travel for three to four months at a time). The last time I opened the sediment filter, the inlet side of the filter element was covered with a fine, silt-like material. Sediment clung to the interior walls of the filter canister. The outlet side of the filter element, however, was clean. The sediment filter had successfully kept that stuff out of our RV's water system.

We would recommend that every RVer at least put a sediment filter on their outside water hose.

Water Heater

We take the convenience of today's RV appliances for granted. Push a button, turn a switch, they work. Most of our RV appliances, however, began as luxuries. The water heater is a great example.

RVers used to heat water in a large kettle on the stove or traipse to the campground rest room and fill their kettle from the washtub's hot water faucet.

Early RV water heaters were cantankerous, propane fueled miniatures of the water heaters in our homes. To light them you went outside (in the rain), kneeled in the mud, opened the outside access door to the water heater, turned a valve to "pilot," held down a red button and attempted (in a howling windstorm) to simultaneously heat a thermocouple and light a pilot flame with a wooden match. On a good day, a skilled RVer could accomplish this feat with less than five matches. Once the pilot was lit, you could turn the valve to "on" and ignite a roaring blowtorch-like flame that would heat the water. When the water reached a predetermined temperature, the "blowtorch" shut off but (with luck and only mild winds) the pilot light continued to burn. When the water temperature dropped, the blowtorch automatically relit to reheat the water. What a great invention!

Some RVers discovered that, once the water in the tank was hot, they could conserve propane by returning the valve to the "pilot" position. The pilot flame by itself would keep the water in the water heater at an acceptably warm temperature.

Today, the same blowtorch heats essentially the same water heater. The big difference is that when you want to light the water heater you simply press the water heater's on/off switch located inside the RV. The blowtorch is automatically ignited. The guy who came up with that improvement has my nomination for the RV Hall Of Fame.

If you want to conserve the propane used by your automatic water heater, turn it off until you actually need hot water. Next time you turn on your water heater, pay attention to how long it takes before it shuts itself off. It shouldn't take more than 20 to 30 minutes to heat a six-gallon water heater.

Rather than listen to our water heater consume propane as it cycles on and off all night, we turn it off. In the morning, we turn on the water heater, plug in the coffee and, if necessary, turn on the furnace. A half-hour later the rig is warm, our coffee is done and our shower water is ready. After showers and breakfast dishes, the water heater is turned off.

Chances are, the only time we will need hot water during the rest of the day is for dinner dishes. Rather than use the amount of propane it would take to heat six gallons of water, we fill a large kettle with water. The kettle is placed on the stove when we sit down for dinner. By the time we are through eating, the hot water for doing dishes is ready.

You may have a combination gas/electric water heater. When you have an electric hookup an electric heating element inside the water heater heats the water. That's the good news. The bad news is that some of these heating elements can draw up to 12 to 14 amps of electricity. Check your water heater's instruction manual to see how many amps your water heater uses. If you have a 30 amp electric hookup and your water heater draws 12 amps, that barely leaves you enough amps to operate one more major appliance.

Occasionally, we turn off the water heater's electric heating element during the day when amperage availability is important to us. We turn it on again at night when we go to bed and no other major appliance is operating. In the morning, we have hot water for showers and breakfast dishes.

Chances are you can add an electric heating element to your RV's existing water heater. Look for them in RV accessory stores and catalogs. We had one in our previous rig. It was not difficult to install, drew only 4 amps and took just a little longer to heat the water than our present 12 amp heating element. Another nomination for the RV Hall Of Fame.

Today's RV water heaters are a great convenience. Just press a switch and in a short amount of time you have hot water. But don't forget, if all else fails, you can always get hot water from the restroom's wash tub or heat it in a kettle on your stove.

Holding Tank Odors

Holding tank odors. Those three words are guaranteed to get the attention of every RVer. We all want to know the magical formula for preventing holding tank odors, eliminating holding tank odors, or both.

Understanding the source of the odors makes it easier to prevent and deal with them.

RVs are equipped with two holding tanks, a gray-water tank and a black-water tank. Properly sealed and vented, holding tanks should not allow odors to escape into the RV.

The gray-water tank captures the waste water from the sinks and shower. The water flows from the drain, through a p-trap and into the gray-water holding tank.

You can see a p-trap under the kitchen sink. It is a u-shaped piece of pipe that retains about a cup-full of drain water. The water trapped in the bottom of the u-shaped pipe prevents gas (and odor) from escaping the holding tank and getting into the RV through the sink drain opening.

The water in the p-trap can evaporate, get splashed out during travel or it can even be sucked out by the vacuum created when the holding tank is drained. When this happens, odors from the holding tank can make their way into the RV by way of the sink or shower drains.

When you smell holding-tank odors, suspect the p-traps first. If the p-trap is the culprit, pouring a cup or two of water into the sink and shower drains will stop the odor. Don't overlook the p-trap for the washer/dryer. Pour some water into the standing drain pipe to refill the washer's p-trap.

While you are looking under the sink, follow the drain pipe. It should make a tee-connection to a vertical pipe. The drain water follows this pipe down into the gray-water holding tank. If the top of the vertical pipe ends in a small cap-like object, that is a one-way check valve. It is supposed to let air into the pipe while water is draining. It should not, however, let air (and odor) out of the pipe.

A defective check valve could be the source of the holding-tank odor. A temporary "band-aid" of duct tape can be applied over the check valve's openings to block the flow of odor until a repair can be effected.

If the vertical pipe goes up through the roof, it doubles as a vent pipe for the holding tank. Every holding tank will have at least one vent pipe. The idea of a vent pipe is to allow air out of the tank as the tank fills and to let air into the tank as the tank empties. Holding-tank gases (and odors) also use the vent pipe to escape into the atmosphere above the RV's roofline.

Incidentally, in the old days, when sewer hoses just lay on the ground instead of on neat looking trestles, RVers would place a short length of 4-by-4 or a rock under the sewer hose. This created an upside-down U that trapped water in the sewer hose between the RV and the sewer inlet. It prevented sewer gas from entering the gray-water tank (and possibly the RV) by way of the sewer hose.

If the holding tank is not properly sealed where the vent pipe enters the holding tank; if the area around the vent pipe is not sealed where it penetrates the roof; or if the pipe is cracked, then holding tank odors can escape into the RV. You might want to have a qualified RV service technician check out these possibilities.

Occasionally, gas from a holding-tank's roof vent can flow across the roof and enter the RV through the roof's air vent. All you can do is shut the air vent and wait for the wind to change direction.

In most RVs, toilet waste goes directly from the toilet bowl into the holding tank without benefit of a trap. The black-water holding tank captures and retains toilet waste.

When the sliding valve at the bottom of the toilet bowl is opened to empty the bowl, a small amount of odor can enter the RV from the holding tank. This is not uncommon when the toilet room's exhaust fan is operating and there are no windows open for the exhaust fan to draw air through. The exhaust fan draws air (and odors) from the holding tank through the open toilet-bowl valve. Be sure a window is open any time an exhaust fan is operating.

If the closed toilet-bowl valve fails to keep water in the toilet bowl, that is another likely opening for sewer gas to enter the RV.

Odors can escape from the black-water holding tank if the toilet-to-holding-tank connection is not properly sealed. And, if the holding-tank vent pipe is not properly sealed at the holding tank, or where the pipe exits through the roof, or if the vent pipe is cracked, odors can make their way into the RV.

Another location where holding tank odors can enter the RV is the toilet overflow drain openings. This is such a common occurrence for some RV toilets that plugs have been designed to seal their openings.

Keep in mind that properly sealed and vented holding tanks will not allow odors to escape into the RV. Whenever you detect holding tank odors, check the holding tank seals and venting system.

Holding-tank odors are a natural result of bacteria trapped inside the tank. Overpowering odors, however, are the result of holding tank solids that remain after the tanks are emptied. Proper draining, rinsing and cleaning can keep holding tank odors to a minimum. And, as previously stated, these odors should not enter the RV if the holding tanks are properly sealed and vented.

Ideally, both holding tanks should not be emptied until they are at least one-half to two-thirds full. This volume of liquid creates a flushing action that washes out most of the solids when the tanks are emptied.

In reality, though, most of us leave our gray-water tank valve open when we have a sewer hookup. This allows grease, oils, bits of food, toothpaste and other things to cling to the floor and walls of the tank and become havens for odor causing bacteria.

And, many of us are in the habit of emptying the black-water tank before going down the road. We do not want to carry any unnecessary weight, and who knows when we will have another chance to empty our holding tanks. Our black-water tank is frequently less than half-full when we empty it. This lack of volume provides an opportunity for bacteria-growing solid matter to remain in the tank.

If the solids in either tank are allowed to dry, they cling to the walls and floor like low-grade cement. They become particularly odorous and difficult to remove.

The key to removing waste and odor causing bacteria from holding tanks is water. Lots and lots of water.

If your gray-water tank has been open while you had a sewer connection, close the valve a day or so before emptying your black-water holding tank. The idea is to capture a sufficient volume of water to help flush out any remaining solids. It will also give you some gray water to flush out the sewer hose after you drain the black-water tank.

When you want to empty a black-water tank that is not yet half full, add liquid by pouring a few buckets of water through the toilet and into the tank.

After draining the black-water tank, and with the valve still open, dump a couple buckets of water through the toilet to help flush out any remaining particles. Close the Black-water tank valve and drain the gray-water tank.

After emptying the holding tanks, close their valves and add a few gallons of water to cover the bottoms of both tanks. This should discourage any remaining waste from solidifying.

Once in a while, after emptying the tanks and before traveling down the road, put five or ten gallons of water into each tank. The traveling motion will slosh the water around the insides of the tanks. Drain the tanks when you arrive at your destination. You have just rinsed out your holding tanks.

An occasional high-pressure rinse can be obtained by using a special wand that connects to a garden hose. The wand is inserted through the toilet into the holding tank. You rotate the wand to aim a high-pressure stream of water at the walls of the tank. Look for these wands where RV accessories are sold.

Rinse and drain both holding tanks before putting your RV into storage. Store the RV with both holding-tank valves open and the drain-valve cover off. This will allow the tanks to dry and prevent the growth of bacteria. You can keep insects and critters out of the tanks by covering the valve opening with aluminum window screen.

The magical formula for preventing holding tank odors from entering your RV is a properly sealed holding-tank system and lots of water.

Jury Duty

" Is there some provision in the law to excuse us from jury duty when we are traveling?"

Joe: All of the juror summons Vicki and I have received during the past eight years have been for dates when we were scheduled to be out of the state.

Contact your local county court system to determine how potential juror lists are drawn up. We understand that most counties rely upon voter registration rolls and/or driver's license lists. Your county courthouse should also be able to give you a specific answer to your question.

Vicki: Each time we have received a jury summons, we have asked for, and been granted, an extension until the date we would return from our travels.

When requesting an extension, we have always told them what dates we would be available for jury duty. An example of our standard response is, "Contractual obligations will keep me out of state until April 13. I will be available for jury duty between April 15 and June 1." In all cases the extension was granted and we were advised to report on the 15th of April.

Joe: Your question does bring up a serious consideration for full-timers who are selecting a state for their home base. Will the local court system react reasonably to a request for changes in the dates of jury duty? I would hate to be pulled away from Florida's sunshine because some court in Alaska insisted I show up for jury duty in the middle of January. And guess who would have to pay for air fare.

Deterring Critters

"We seem to be having a lot of trouble with ants getting into our trailer. Any thoughts on how to discourage critters and pests from entering RVs?"

Vicki: Try to locate and seal off the openings that could allow those unwelcome visitors to enter your rig.

One way to do this is to wait until it's dark outside. Open and illuminate all the interior closets and cabinets next to the floor. Now check under the outside of the RV to see if any light is coming through.

Conversely, you can also light up the outside of the RV and see if you can find any light making its way into the darkened interior of the coach.

Follow plumbing and wiring to where it passes through floors and walls. Do this both inside and outside. Once you have located all the potential entryways, seal them by injecting some Styrofoam into the openings (you can get spray cans of Styrofoam at your hardware store). Not too much, though. The Styrofoam expands after it leaves the can and a little goes a long way.

The advantage to using Styrofoam is that it won't damage anything and it can be easily removed if the plumbing or wiring has to be worked on.

Closing these openings will not only help keep out critters, it will seal out dust and moisture as well.

Occasionally you'll camp in an area where ants know how to get into RVs. When it looks like ants might be a problem, we spread a small amount of borax powder or kitchen cleanser containing bleach around the tires, leveling jacks and any other items on the RV that contact the ground. Ants don't seem to want to cross this stuff.

We also smear about a one-inch band of petroleum jelly around our electrical cord, water hose and sewer hose to discourage ants from using them as a bridge to our RV. Joe tries to tell people that it makes the hose slippery and the ants plunge to their death. Whatever it does, it works.

Mothballs will ward off ants, mice and spiders. Spiders are attracted to the smell of propane so we place a few mothballs in our refrigerator and water heater's outside access compartments.

We've also been told that fabric sofener sheets repel mice. I won't tell you Joe's theory on that one.

Don't overlook the pest products you can find in hardware, garden and grocery stores.

Condensation

"We are having a lot of problems with condensation on the windows of our RV. The problem is especially bad in the mornings. How do we stop this from happening?"

Vicki: Condensation occurs when the warm, moist, interior air of the RV comes in contact with a cool surface. Not only does it happen on the windows and mirrors but the interior walls as well.

Moisture in the air comes from a variety of sources. Cooking, showering, even breathing are just a few.

The trick to minimizing condensation is to eliminate or reduce the moisture in the air.

Turn on a nearby exhaust fan when cooking, washing dishes or showering. This will remove the moist air before it mixes with the air in the rest of the RV.

Keep your roof vents cracked open. This will allow moist air to escape.

Open a window to exchange humid interior air with dry outside air. Even when it's raining, the air inside your RV can be more humid than it is outside.

Joe: We keep a window open at least a half inch at each end of our RV. We also leave the center roof vent open. Sometimes we operate the roof-vent fan at low speed.

When cooking creates a lot of steam or when we have guests generating a lot of hot air, the windows are opened wider and the speed of the fan increased.

Try different combinations of opening windows, opening roof vents and operating exhaust fans to reduce the moisture and thus the condensatrion inside your RV.

Smoke Odors

"We purchased a fifth wheel trailer from a couple who apparently were heavy smokers. We have been unable to eliminate the odor of tobacco smoke. We have washed everything thoroughly and shampooed the carpet. Still, the odor remains. We prefer not to just cover up the smell but to remove it completely. We would appreciate any solutions you may have."

Vicki: Here are some home remedies that RVers have suggested will remove the odor of tobacco smoke. We haven't tried any of them but they appear harmless. You might try them one at a time.

Mix a half-cup of vinegar with a half-cup of water and bring to a boil. Leave them out to evaporate in the RV.

Sprinkle cinnamon on a pan and warm it on the stove.

Place a tablespoon or two of cinnamon in a pan of water and bring to a boil.

Mix vinegar, cinnamon and a few cloves in small jars. Microwave the open jars for a minute and place them throughout the RV.

Heat a couple of teaspoons of peanut butter in a frying pan for a few minutes.

Joe: If cooking salad dressing doesn't do the trick, you might contact a company that handles fire and water damage restoration. Look for them in your yellow pages or ask your insurance agent for a recommendation. These folks deal with smoke odors by thoroughly washing everything. Then, inside the closed RV, they either vaporize a deodorizer for 20 to 30 minutes or run an ozone machine for 24 to 48 hours.

Best Dogs For RVing

"We travel in our RV for two to three months at a time. Our last dog just happened to love RVing as much as we do. It's time to get another and I was wondering what size or type dog might be best for RVing."

Joe: There must be an unwritten rule that states the size of the dog should be inversely proportionate to the size of the RV. Next time you are in a campground, see if the St. Bernard doesn't belong to the owner of the van camper. And notice the size of the dog sitting in the pocket of the person that just got out of the 40-foot fifth-wheeler. Go figure!

It only make sense for RVers to consider the size of the dog that will share their traveling home. A pet, its bed, food and water bowls, leash, scooper, toys, grooming equipment, food and other paraphernalia is going to take up precious space.

An RVing dog is going to spend the majority of its time inside. It is going to have to sleep, eat and just "hang out" somewhere. So, yes, size of the dog is an important consideration.

But don't let size be the only factor. There are some high-energy breeds of small dogs whose activity level takes up considerably more space than their larger more laid-back cousins.

An animal's energy level is also going to dictate the amount of daily exercise it will require. And you know who is going to be on the other end of that leash.

Vicki: While you are walking that dog, how is it going to react when approached by strange dogs, people and children? Some breeds simply do not do well here.

Pay attention to the temperament and especially the reputation of the breed of dog you choose. Rotweilers and Pit Bulls, deservedly or not, are specifically prohibited from some otherwise pet-friendly RV parks.

Some breeds have a reputation for being sweet and lovable as long as you are present. When you leave without them, they become the dogs from Hades. They bark incessantly, tear up the furniture and forget all the pleasant hours you spent house breaking them.

Joe: Speaking of hot places, how will the dog tolerate temperature extremes? Many short haired varieties really suffer in cold weather.

What reaction will they have to going into strange places? We once had a dog that refused to go potty anywhere but her own back yard. One time she held back for a week before we finally broke down and returned home. I thought her eyes would never uncross.

Do they train easily? Golden Retrievers can't please you fast enough. Dachshunds believe that it is you who needs training. (We've had both.)

And then there are dogs with a constant puddle under their jaws, oily hair, bad breath, body odor, and who shed enough hair to stuff a pillow.

Vicki: The point is, some breeds of dogs will do better in an RVing environment than others. Research the different breeds at the library or on the internet (www.dogbreedinfo.com is a good start). Be sure you choose a dog that will enjoy RVing as much as you do.

Generating Income

"Is there some way I can generate income while RVing? Can I get work while traveling in my RV? Can I operate a business on the road? Can I make money on the road?"

Joe: We hear these questions with more frequency these days. Those who ask come from a variety of RV lifestyles. Young couples dreaming of adventure. Middle age folks burned out by the rat race. Retirees looking for a way to supplement their incomes.

Yes, we tell them. Yes, you can get work. Yes, you can operate a business on the road. Yes, you can make money while RVing!

We are prime examples of making money on the road. Since 1989 we have worked exhibit booths at RV shows, escorted RV caravans to Mexico and Alaska, sold books, taught RVing classes, written magazine articles and presented seminars at RV events.

Along the way, we have met hundreds of other RVers who combined RV travel with making money.

We met a man in an RV park who was making a casual dollar. He made ornamental airplanes out of aluminum beer cans. Half a dozen different styles hung from his awning. The slightest breeze would set the propellers to spinning. He sat under his awning fashioning airplanes while simultaneously creating empty beer cans. There were no signs, but for $7.00 he could be talked into giving you one (an airplane, that is). Not only was he making a casual dollar; he was obviously enjoying what he was doing.

Lots of RVers spend their RV vacations searching for antiques, collectibles and other items they can sell at garage sales and flea markets.

There is the couple who make unusual Christmas tree ornaments from driftwood, sea shells, pine cones and other of nature's castaways. Their vacations and weekends are spent gathering their raw materials. They sell the ornaments to Christmas boutiques

We have run across a number of folks who pick up occasional cash by selling crafts, hand-made jewelry and other items at flea markets.

Now, none of these folks are going to pay for their travels or make a payment on their RV with their earnings. But they have found a way to make a casual dollar by pursuing the kinds of activities that interest them. Can your hobby or favorite pastime be turned into a money-making endeavor?

Vicki: Many retired RVers offset their travel expenses by being campground hosts. Campground hosts at government campgrounds typically receive a free campsite, usually with full hookups, in exchange for about 20 hours a week of light work.

Government campground host duties vary depending upon the campground. Generally, they consist of greeting and providing information to campers, light housekeeping chores and minor maintenance duties.

Commercial campgrounds and RV parks may offer more responsible duties accompanied by modest salaries. Jobs include office work, security, recreation and maintenance.

The best part of campground hosting is that the jobs are available during the most pleasant times of the year. RVers can find hosting positions in the north during the summer and in the south during the winter.

The concessionaires at National Parks hire thousands of RVers to operate their hotels, gas stations, grocery stores, gift shops and restaurants. Every summer the concessionaire literally opens up an entire city. Jobs include personnel clerks, managers, supervisors, electricians, carpenters, drivers, tour guides, security, medical personnel; the list goes on.

A few years ago we visited a national park during the fall. It was obvious the concessionaire was preparing to close for the winter. During a walk through the campground we happened upon a group of partying employees. Knowing how difficult it can be working with the public, we asked if they were celebrating the end of having to deal with tourists. "Oh," one replied, "the tourists aren't that bad. We're just saying farewell to the good friends we've made while working here this summer. Tomorrow, six of us are caravanning to Florida. We have jobs waiting that will take us through the winter."

Joe: RVers can supplement their existing income a number of ways while traveling.

We met a woman who specialized in doing portraits of couples standing in front of their RVs. She would take a Polaroid photo of the couple and work from that. She would sit under her awning while she painted. Obviously, she attracted a lot of attention. Passing campers would see her work and ask if she would do a portrait of them or their grandchildren or their pet. Pet lovers were among her best customers.

Street artists do portraits or caricatures at fairs, RV shows and other events just as they do on street corners. Musicians, magicians, mimes, clowns and entertainers can also be found working at these same crowd gathering events. What better way for an itinerant entertainer to travel than in an RV?

Most of the folks working the exhibit booths at RV shows are, themselves, RVers. Some are professional pitch people. They sell pots and pans, solar panels and gadgets. Usually on a commission basis. Others are there to hand out literature or make you aware of a product. They receive a daily fee or salary.

We know one full-timing couple who supplement their retirement by selling RV water filters at RV shows, rallies and fairs. Their inventory and display materials travel in their motorhome's storage bays.

Sometimes they set up under the awning of their rig; other times they set up inside a tent or building set aside for the vendors.

It took a few years of trial and error but these folks had established a circuit of the shows, rallies and fairs that are most likely to turn a profit for them.

Many RVers get temporary jobs on the road. Construction booms seem to move around the country. If you have a skill or trade associated with construction or real estate you can use your RV to follow the booms.

Vicki: Seasonal jobs are natural income opportunities for RVers. Pumpkin lots and Christmas tree lots are frequently staffed by RVers. Oftentimes the owner is thrilled to have these conscientious employees stay in their rigs right on the lot.

Christmas season sees the demand for stock handlers, sales clerks and gift wrappers. And somebody must be painting those greetings and decorations on the store windows.

Tax preparers are busy from January through the middle of April. Many tax preparation companies offer training free or at nominal cost.

Don't overlook the temporary help agencies. Employers are turning to temp agencies for engineers, nurses, draftsmen, accountants, computer operators and all kinds of employees.

A retired police officer went to a temp agency that has branches nationwide. He established himself as an honest, reliable security guard with that office. Then he began his RV travels. Whenever he wants to pick up a little extra income, he goes to a branch of that temp agency. At first, copies of his performance records were faxed from one branch to the other. Today they are in a central computer. His track record allows him to pick his days and hours.

Yes, you can make money while you travel. But, like all decisions related to RVing, you will have to compromise. You will have to decide how much time you want devote to making money and how much time you want to spend enjoying your travels.

Travel vibrations can cause aluminum drink cans to leave black marks on the interior walls and shelves of the refrigerator. You can prevent this by using a plastic storage box (without the lid) as a drink-can container inside your refrigerator.

RV Caravans

"We have been RVing for a couple of years now. So far our camping trips have been local ones. My husband will retire this fall and we want to travel around the United States, Canada and Mexico. The RV caravan ads look appealing. But we wonder if we should have more travel experience before joining one. What do you think?"

Joe: It appears that you are comfortable with driving, operating and camping in your RV. An RV caravan would be a great introduction to the joys of extended RV travel.

Caravan companies research, organize and conduct escorted tours for the enjoyment of RVers. As a caravan participant you will have the comfort of traveling and living in your own rig, the convenience of professionals making all the arrangements and the confidence that nothing will be missed along the way. You will also have the sense of camaraderie and security that comes from traveling with a group of fellow RVers.

Depending upon the destination and activities, caravans can last from two to ten weeks. RV caravans are offered to destinations throughout the United States, Canada and Mexico. Caravans, in rented RVs, are even available to Europe, Australia and New Zealand.

Vicki: After signing on for a caravan you will receive information, maps, itineraries and checklists to help you prepare for the journey.

Caravans rendezvous at a convenient starting point. A day or two is spent inspecting rigs, making last minute preparations and getting acquainted with fellow caravaners.

The caravan staff typically consists of a wagonmaster couple and an assistant wagonmaster couple. The wagonmasters' responsibility is to keep the caravan running smoothly. The assistant wagonmasters assist where needed. Sometimes the assistants are referred to as tailgunners. One of their responsibilities may be to remain behind the last RV so they can assist in the event of a breakdown.

A travel day might begin with a briefing conducted by the wagonmaster. You will hear about the day's travel route, interesting side trips, scenic attractions and points of interest.

Your tour map and itinerary will be complemented by the wagonmaster's briefing. Some maps will even show where fuel and propane may be purchased.

A day's journey, typically about 200 miles, may include a rendezvous for lunch or a guided tour. It's not unusual for many tours to be conducted on chartered buses, boats and trains.

Upon reaching the day's destination, the caravan staffers will guide you to your reserved campsite. Evening meals on a caravan can be anything from a cookout on a sandy beach to a colorful fiesta. Spontaneous fresh-caught fish dinners and occasional pot lucks are inevitable and festive get togethers. Your RV kitchen is always available for your favorite home-cooked meal and restaurants are usually available nearby if you want to sample some local food.

Caravaning isn't necessarily for everyone. Positives for some can be perceived as negatives by others. Campground reservations and ferry timetables require adherence to travel schedules. Shared laughter and adventures involve group participation. The security and camaraderie of group travel calls for consideration and compromise.

Joe: To learn more about RV caravans contact several caravan companies. You will find a number of them advertising in RV magazines. Do not overlook the Good Sam Club. They have been conducting RV caravans throughout the United States, Canada and Mexico for years.

Compare what the different caravan companies have to offer. How long have they been in business? How many times have they conducted the tour you are interested in? What, specifically, will you get for your money? Ask for a detailed description of the activities, tours and events included in the price of the caravan. How many RVs will be in the caravan? How many staff members? What kind of campgrounds will you stay in? Will they have hookups? Who pays for ferries, trains and other forms of transportation. What optional activities and costs are involved? Ask about the experience of the wagonmasters. Request the names and phone numbers of recent caravan customers. Call and ask those customers what they liked best and what they liked least about the caravan company, the caravan and the wagonmasters.

Vicki: Caravans can be a great introduction to RV travel. We would particularly encourage anyone contemplating their first RV trip to Mexico to seriously consider the benefits of caravan travel.

Simple Solutions

In this age of high-tech we sometimes forget to look for simple solutions. Not long ago we watched a camper spend a lot of time assembling a set of giant Legos into a leveling ramp. He placed the ramp in front of the tire on the low side of his trailer. After a few trial and error attempts, he managed to pull his trailer up onto enough Legos to get level.

A few minutes later, another trailerist pulled into the adjoining site. After sizing up the situation he used the side of his shoe to scrape an indentation into the ground in front of the tire on the high side of his trailer. Then he pulled forward, the tire rolled into the indentation and the trailer was level. A simple solution.

Here are a few other simple solutions:

Situation: You position your RV in the campsite and get it level. That's when you discover you have parked just close enough to a tree or the hookup station to prevent you from completely opening your slideout room or a side-cabinet door (usually the one your hookup stuff is in).

Solution: Most RVers have a metal rod they use to open and close their RV's awning. That awning rod can double as a measuring stick. Measure the distance you need from the wall of your RV to open the side cabinet door and/or slideout room. Mark that distance on the awning rod with a piece of bright colored tape. Before pulling into the campsite, place the awning rod on the ground; one end of the rod touching the tree or other obstacle, the other end (with the bright colored tape) extending into the campsite. As you move your RV into the site, use the awning rod as a guide to give your slideout the room it needs.

An alternative to the awning rod is a brightly colored yardstick cut to the appropriate length.

Situation: Connecting a drinking-water hose to a campground water hydrant can be a challenge if the hose fitting does not turn easily.

Solution: Instead, attach your water-pressure regulator directly to the campground hydrant. It is larger than the hose fitting and easier to handle. The water-pressure regulator will now protect your hose as well as your RV's plumbing. Place "quick-connect" water-hose fittings on the water-pressure regulator and all your hose ends. Now it is literally a snap to connect or disconnect the hose, water-pressure regulator, outside water filter and/or other hoses.

When you disconnect from the campground hydrant, drain the hose as you coil it, then connect both ends to keep any remaining moisture in as well as dirt and critters out.

Situation: Drinking water hoses are sold in 25-foot lengths. You do not always need 25 feet of hose.

Solution: Cut a 25-foot length of hose into ten and fifteen-foot lengths. Using a hose repair kit, install the appropriate male or female hose fittings on the cut ends of the hose. Attach quick-connect fittings to each end of both hoses. Now you have your choice of using a 10-foot, 15-foot and, by joining them together, a 25 foot length of hose. Add an extra 25- foot hose to your collection, and you will be able to reach out as far as 50 feet to a water hydrant.

Situation: Switching the sewer-inlet adapter back and forth between the 10 and 20-foot sewer hoses is a lot of bother. Leaving it on the 20-foot hose often results in ten or more feet of excess sewer hose snaking around the hookup area.

Solution: Similar to the water hose situation above. Cut about a two-foot length from a 10-foot sewer hose. Attach the sewer-inlet adapter to one end of the two-foot section and a female sewer-hose fitting to the other end. Attach a male sewer-hose fitting to one end of the remaining 8-foot hose and a female sewer-hose fitting to the other end. Attach male and female sewer-hose fittings to the ends of the 20-foot sewer hose.

Now you can easily couple the sewer-inlet adapter to either the 8-foot or the 20-foot hose. You can also couple the two hoses together and create a 30-footer.

Situation: Its difficult to slip the sewer-hose fittings into the end of the sewer hose.

Solution: Dip the end of the hose into a bucket of hot water for a minute or so. The hot water will soften the hose and make it easier to slip in the fitting.

Some RVers claim they stretch the warm sewer hose by forcing it over a wine bottle. This may just be an excuse to empty the wine bottle first.

Don't forget to put the loose retainer ring on the hose before attaching the fitting.

Situation: Your RV's 30-amp cord, one end of which is hard wired to the RV, is difficult to coil and store.

Solution: Stand at the RV end of the cord and coil it by pulling the campground end towards you.

Situation: Your RV is parked on a paved campsite that isn't level.

Solution: Get a set of giant Legos...

Into The 20th Century

"When are you going to join the twentieth century and get an e-mail address?"

Joe: Haven't you noticed? This is a decidedly non-technical column. Vicki and I are living proof that you do not have to be a rocket scientist to enjoy RVing.

Believe it or not, our motorhome does not have a satellite dish, GPS system or solar panels. Television is not important (or appealing) enough for us to mess with setting up a satellite dish. We have successfully traveled all over the North American continent using Auto Club maps. And our batteries have never been depleted.

We have pounded out this column for five years on a computer with a 25 megahertz microprocessor. That qualifies it for the Smithsonian but it sure beats a typewriter. And, as far as e-mail goes, your letter arrived just fine via the US Postal Service.

Vicki: Forgive him. Joe recently mourned the arrival of his 60th birthday. He thinks he is supposed to talk like an old fogey. Joe forgot to mention that he successfully mastered the push button phone, automatic teller machine and VCR a long time ago. Although I did have to keep our kids out of hearing distance while he did.

And, as much as he loves that old PC, when we are on the road each of us uses a modern laptop computer. All of our columns and articles are e-mailed to the magazine editors. In fact, when we can't find a telephone hookup in a campground, Joe connects our laptop to our cellular telephone and transmits our e-mail that way. So, in fairness to the old man, Joe, kicking and screaming, has joined the 20th century.

Have you discovered the joys of the internet. Surely you have seen our RV Insight column in the Good Sam website (www.goodsamclub.com). It's interesting how people use the internet. Our daughter is attracted to chat rooms and games. Joe thinks of it as a research tool. I like bumming (surfing) around, discovering interesting websites.

If you enjoy discovering interesting websites, take a look at our new website: www.rv know how.com. It provides us one more avenue to share our 35+ years of RVing experience and knowledge with you. We offer RVing tips, tricks and techniques for both the beginning and seasoned RVer. Check it out, let us know what you think.

Joe: And if you have any comments or questions, there's even an e-mail address.

Enjoy The Journey!

Visit Our Website: www.rv know how.com

An informative website offering practical, useful
articles about RVs, RVers and RVing.

Other Books By Joe and Vicki Kieva

RVing Made Easy

A non-technical book that helps you discover how
easy it is to choose, operate, and enjoy your RV.

Extended RV Travel

Answers questions about choosing an RV, preparing
for and living on the road for weeks/months at a time.

RVing Tips, Tricks And Techniques

This collection of Joe and Vicki Kieva's popular RV
advice columns is a guide for successful RVing.

	Price	Qty	Total
RVing Made Easy	$12.95		$
Extended RV Travel	$12.95		$
RVing Tips, Tricks	$12.95		$
Shipping (USA, $2.00) (Canada $3.50)			$
Total (Please send check or money order in US funds)			$

Your Name_____

Address_____

City_____ State _____ Zip _____

Mail to: RV Travel Adventures
             P.O. Box 5055
             Huntington Beach, Ca 92615

Visit Our Website: www.rv know how.com

> An informative website offering practical, useful
> articles about RVs, RVers and RVing.

Other Books By Joe and Vicki Kieva

RVing Made Easy
A non-technical book that helps you discover how
easy it is to choose, operate, and enjoy your RV.

Extended RV Travel
Answers questions about choosing an RV, preparing
for and living on the road for weeks/months at a time.

RVing Tips, Tricks And Techniques
This collection of Joe and Vicki Kieva's popular RV
advice columns is a guide for successful RVing.

	Price	Qty	Total
RVing Made Easy	$12.95	_____	$ _____
Extended RV Travel	$12.95	_____	$ _____
RVing Tips, Tricks	$12.95	_____	$ _____
Shipping (USA, $2.00) (Canada $3.50)			$ _____

Total (Please send check or money order in US funds) $ _____

Your Name _____

Address _____

City _____ State _____ Zip _____

Mail to: RV Travel Adventures
           P.O. Box 5055
           Huntington Beach, Ca 92615